EVERYDAY
SURVIVAL
HACKS

Quick Fixes to Save

Time and Money

and Avoid Daily Disasters

Reader's
Digest

A READER'S DIGEST BOOK

Copyright © 2020 Trusted Media Brands, Inc.

All rights reserved. Unauthorized reproduction, in any manner, is prohibited.

Reader's Digest is a registered trademark of Trusted Media Brands, Inc.

Cover illustrations by godfather744431/Shutterstock.com
Interior illustrations by Shintayu Layung Sinawang

ISBN 978-1-62145-492-2

Portions of this book were previously published in *Don't Screw It Up!* and *Avoiding Everyday Disasters*.

We are committed to both the quality of our products and the service we provide to our customers.
We value your comments, so please feel free to contact us.

Reader's Digest Adult Trade Publishing
44 South Broadway
White Plains, NY 10601

For more Reader's Digest products and information, visit our website:
www.rd.com (in the United States)
www.readersdigest.ca (in Canada)

Printed in the United States

1 3 5 7 9 10 8 6 4 2

NOTES TO OUR READERS

The information in this book should not be substituted for, or used to alter, medical therapy without your doctor's advice. For a specific health problem, consult your physician for guidance.

All do-it-yourself activities involve a degree of risk. Skills, materials, tools, and site conditions vary widely. Although the editors have made every effort to ensure accuracy, the reader remains responsible for the selection and use of tools, materials, and methods. Always obey local codes and laws, follow manufacturer's operating instructions, and observe safety precautions.

Reader's Digest publishes the advice of expert authorities in many fields. But the use of a book is not a substitute for legal, accounting, or other professional services. Consult a competent professional for answers to your specific questions. This publication is sold with the understanding that the contributors and the publisher are not engaged in rendering legal advice. Laws vary from state to state, and readers with specific issues should seek the services of an attorney.

Products or active ingredients, treatments, and the names of organizations that appear in this publication are included for informational purposes only; the inclusion of commercial products in the book does not imply endorsement by Reader's Digest, nor does the omission of any product or active ingredient or treatment advice indicate disapproval by Reader's Digest. When using any commercial product, readers should read and follow all label directions carefully. The publisher and the contributors specifically disclaim any responsibility for any liability, loss, or risk (personal, financial, or otherwise) that may be claimed or incurred as a consequence, directly or indirectly, of the use and/or application of any of the contents of this publication.

CONTENTS

EVERYDAY
SURVIVAL
HACKS

TIDYING UP

1 **Double up on your welcome mats.** A nice welcome mat gives guests a place to wipe their feet—but a second mat inside the door will catch a lot of the dirt they knocked loose outside. Be sure to shake the dirt off of welcome mats from time to time; otherwise, you're just giving your guests a place to pick up debris to track around your house!

2 **Consider adopting a shoes-off policy.** Getting into the habit of removing shoes at the door will keep your family from tracking dirt into the house. Keep a pair of slippers for each family member near the door, so you can change from your outdoor to your indoor footwear.

3 **Choose the broom your floor wants.** Brooms for the house come in two basic designs: made with either soft plastic bristles or straw. Straw brooms are best for rough, worn flooring, but they are too harsh for delicate finishes. If your floor is new and (as yet) undamaged, you'll want to use a plastic model to keep it that way.

4 **Sweep thoroughly.** Select a broom with an angled head if you need to get under cabinets. Before sweeping, don't forget to turn off any fans or other devices that might blow the dust around the room. Got a little line of dirt that just won't get into the dustpan? Pull out your hand vacuum and suck it up, or use a moistened towel to mop up the dirt's last line of defense.

5 **Strategize your sweep.** If your room is square, use the perimeter method. Pick one corner and sweep inward along the walls. Then work around the room, spiraling inward, until you have a neat little pile of dirt in the middle of the room. If your room is more rectangular, start at one end and work toward the other. You'll end up with a series of small dirt piles at the end of each row, which you can combine into one at the very end.

6 **Absorb household odors with coffee.** Keep an open can of ground coffee near the cat's litter box, or in the corner of the laundry room. Your nose will thank you!

7 **Shellac the walls to seal away bad smells.** Walls are particularly absorbent of smoke and other odors. If yours are giving you trouble, you can try implementing the technique experts use in buildings that have absorbed smoke from fires. After you seal the walls and ceilings with shellac or a shellac-based primer—this helps lock in the odor—then repaint.

8 **Charcoal rids a room of paint fumes.** Place a few charcoal briquettes in a pan in the center of a newly painted room, and close the door. The smell will be gone soon—sometimes within a day!

9 **Leave the dishwashing to the dishwasher.**
Don't rinse your dishes before you put them in—
besides wasting water, it's bad for your dishes.
Dishwashing detergent was created to dissolve
food, and if it's in there without food to dissolve, it
will start attacking the dishes and glassware.

10 **Don't overdo it on dishwashing detergent.**
Dishwashers use less water than they did in days
gone by, and detergents are more concentrated.
This means you need less soap. Otherwise, not
only are you spending more than you have to on
something that's (literally) going down the drain—
but also, too much soap leads to cloudy glasses.

11 **Use vinegar to clean your dishwasher.** Are your
dishes coming out of the dishwasher with a frosty
white film on them? This is a residue of minerals
that new phosphate-free detergents can leave
behind. Try this mineral-removing trick to get your
dishwasher back to normal: Put two cups of white
vinegar into a bowl and place it in your dishwasher's
bottom rack. Run the washer without detergent, with
only the bowl of vinegar in it. Once it has completed
its cycle, run it a second time (this time completely
empty) to remove the leftover vinegar.

12 **Load your dishwasher outside-in.** Place large items at the side and back of the dishwasher. This prevents them from keeping water and detergent from reaching other dishes. The dirtier side of each dish should face toward the center, where it'll be more exposed to the spray.

13 **Know your mildews and don'ts.** One of the most common household stinks is caused by mildew, which thrives in areas with prolonged moisture. If you want to prevent it from growing in your bathroom, get the air circulating when all that post-shower steam is in the air. A dehumidifier or an exhaust fan will do the trick. Also, make sure you hang your damp towels so they aren't touching each other—that way they can dry more quickly and thoroughly.

14 **Freshen up your towels.** Mix equal parts Borax and laundry soap, and pour the mixture into the washing machine with the offensive towels. Start the machine on a regular cycle to let it fill with water, then pause the cycle to let the towels (or clothing or shoes) soak for about twenty minutes before you allow it to resume.

15 **Don't mix commercial cleaners.** You may be tempted when you're dealing with stubborn filth that no single product is defeating, but this is a big mistake. Certain cleaning agents, great on their own, can produce dangerous chemical reactions when mixed. Most people have heard not to mix straight ammonia and bleach—the gas can inflame your airways and damage the lining of your lungs. They might not put two and two together about other hazards, though: when blended, the chemicals in that great new toilet cleanser and fantastic toilet scrub can create chlorine gas . . . which can be deadly.

16 **Use spray cleaners sparingly.** More is not always better. Spraying too much cleaner for a job just gives you more junk to wipe up, causing you to waste your energy and money *and* inhale extra chemicals that can give you respiratory problems over time.

PET CARE

1 **To teach your dog to love a bath, take it slowly.** Baths can be a positive place for dogs, and your life will be much easier if your dog is willing to get into the tub himself—especially if he's large! The trick to avoiding bath-time battles is not to spring the idea on your dog all at once. Start with a dry tub, and lure your dog in with a treat. While she's in the tub, play with your dog with a special toy, or pet her and speak in a soothing voice. Then take her back out. A few days later, try doing the same thing with a small amount of water in the tub. Then try it with a little more. Keep the water lukewarm, so that it's comfortable for her. Before you know it, the dog will not only get into a filled tub but let you wet her down without a fuss!

2 **Brush your dog before bathtime.** Brush out your dog's coat thoroughly. You want to be sure all mats have been removed—any remaining knots will become tighter once they're wet.

3 **Refine your dog-drying technique.** Keep the towel close at hand. You don't want to have to hunt for a towel with your dog still in the tub, especially if she's trying to get out. Rather than rubbing your dog dry—which will tangle her fur—pat her dry, and squeeze out any excess water.

4 **Use specially formulated shampoos for your dog.** Don't use the stuff you use on your own hair. Human shampoos have the wrong pH balance for dogs, and can lead to health problems if used.

5 **When bathing your dog, don't skip the hard-to-reach parts.** If you just scrub your dog's back and sides, he isn't really clean. You'll need to wash his underside, where the most dirt collects, and his head and face, too. The bath is also a good time to check your dog's skin for lumps. If you find anything suspicious, have it checked by a vet.

6 **Stay in charge during your dog's bathtime.** If your dog becomes nervous in the bath and tries to make a run for it, you need to be gentle but firm. Don't stop to soothe her; this will only reinforce her anxiety. Instead, keep bathing her while speaking in a calm voice. Once she has calmed down, praise her and maybe even offer her a treat.

7 **Use a handheld showerhead to wash your dog.** Bathing your dog is much easier if you have a handheld showerhead or spray nozzle that attaches to your bath faucet. You can also use a plastic cup to scoop water from the bath, but a spray nozzle does a better job of penetrating fur. (Also, if your dog is quite dirty, scooping bathwater over him will simply be dumping some of the same dirt back onto him!)

8 **Make your furniture less cat-claw-friendly.** Cats like to scratch anything that has a satisfying texture. The wooden legs of your dining-room set or the sides of your upholstered armchair feel especially nice to a cat's claws. One way to make your furniture less appealing is by putting double-faced masking tape or a plastic cover over a favorite scratching spot. You can also use citrus sprays on the furniture—cats hate that stuff!

9 **Keep your cat well (scratch-) posted.** Cats have an innate need to scratch their territory in particular spots, so place a scratching post near any area that your cat loves to claw. Once she has become accustomed to using the post, you should be able to uncover the furniture.

10 **Stay positive with your cat.** Unlike dogs, cats don't respond to negative reinforcement. Yelling may stop your cat from what she's doing at the moment, but it won't teach her to avoid it in the future—and physically reprimanding a cat will never, ever work. The best way to train your cat

to scratch a post and not your couch is by enticing her to do so. Rub some catnip on the post, put some treats around it, and include it in playtime.

HOME UPKEEP

1 **Buy extra wallpaper.** Wallpapering is tricky, and you might screw up with a roll or two before you get the hang of things. You don't want to run out of wallpaper partway through and run back to the store, only to find that your choice is no longer in stock. This is especially true if your paper is from a discontinued line or has a pattern. You're more likely to waste the patterned stuff, because the pattern won't always align perfectly the first time. Finally, double-check to make sure the batch numbers on all of your rolls match, to avoid surrounding yourself with two shades of (almost) the same color.

2 **Dip your paintbrush lightly.** The more paint there is on a paintbrush, the more there is to drip off. For better control, hold the handle close to the brush head, not at the end. As you work, paint will accumulate at the base of the brush; stroke outward from time to time to keep that buildup from dripping all over the place.

3 Screen out lumpy paint. When you open a can of paint, cut out a circle of window-screening material to fit the inside of the can. After stirring the paint, lay the screen over the surface. As the screen sinks, it will carry the lumpy paint particles to the bottom of the can. Don't have any old screens to cut up? You can also buy cheap disposable strainer bags designed for painters.

4 Don't drench the paint roller. For neat paint rolling, bring some paint up into the slanted part of the tray, and use this thin coating to cover your roller. Roll back and forth several times, pressing firmly to make the roller grip the paint. Cover the roller thinly and evenly—if you have excess paint on the surface of the roller, it will not only drip and splatter, but it will also go on the wall unevenly and produce dreaded paint streaks. Roll it onto the wall slowly, and put some muscle into it as you go to ensure even coverage. This is especially important for ceilings. (And if you're painting those, you'd better get some goggles too.)

5 **Make a paint swatch for later.** Before you pack your painting supplies away, cut a smallish piece of cardboard and give it a few coats of paint. Now you have a handy sample of your wall color to take with you when you're shopping for furniture and other decorative items.

6 **Save leftover paint.** To keep leftover paint from drying up in the can, pour it into a smaller airtight container, such as a plastic milk jug that you've rinsed out thoroughly. Remember to label the outside of the container by manufacturer, color, number, and storage date, and store it somewhere as close to room temperature as possible—and where it won't be mistaken for food!

7 **Anchor bigger pictures.** A nail and hook is fine for hanging smaller framed pictures, but if you have a larger frame—and aren't able to nail directly into a stud—you'll need to use hollow-wall anchors. These distribute the frame's weight and grip the drywall more securely than nails.

8 **Hang artwork with an eye for everything else in the room.** Your art will look best if you hang it so that it's centered at approximately eye level and positioned horizontally in keeping with the lines of furniture or windows. One easy way to get an idea of how a picture will look in place is to trace around the picture on a piece of paper, cut it out, and then stick the paper on the wall. And remember: don't hang tiny pictures on a huge wall—they'll look lonely there!

9 **Masking tape keeps pictures straight.** A painting will slide around if the wire is too smooth. You can fix this by wrapping a little masking tape around the part of the wire that goes over the hook. The texture will keep the wire from slipping and leaving you with the dreaded droopy look. For added stability, secure the bottom corners of the frame with poster tack, museum wax, or rubber feet—all of which are available at craft-supply stores.

10 **When diagnosing a sink drip, start small.** Before disassembling your sink, first check to see if you have a blocked aerator. The aerator is a little fixture on the end of your faucet that softens the flow of water by introducing air into the stream. The screen inside can get clogged, causing the faucet to run slowly even when hot and cold are both turned on. It will also trap water that will *drip, drip, drip* once the faucet's turned off. If this is your problem, it's an easy fix: unscrew the aerator, clean out the screen, and put it back on.

11 **Prep wood before driving a screw into it.** To keep from splitting the wood, drill a pilot hole first. Using a drill, an awl, or an ice pick, make a hole slightly smaller than the diameter of the screw—and always use a drill when placing the screw near the end of a board. Another method to prevent splitting is to clamp the edges of the wood before screwing. This reduces outward pressure on the grain, and keeps everything together.

12 **Don't use screwdrivers for other stuff.** People ruin screwdrivers—and injure themselves—by using them for tasks they aren't meant for. One of the most common misuses is using the plastic handle of the screwdriver to whack a nail into place. The plastic is usually not hard enough for this, and can shatter into pieces. Try not to use screwdrivers to pry things up, either. They can snap in half under the pressure, sending you reeling.

13 **Choose the right glue for the job.** There are many different types of glue available, each of which is best suited for a particular material. Fabric glue won't dissolve in water, for example, and decoupage glue is best for a shiny, transparent finish. Choose the appropriate type and applicator for the task at hand, and always read the instructions carefully.

14 **Don't get attached to your superglue.** When using superglue, cover your work surface with cloth or metal foil. This will prevent any spilled glue from remaining on the work surface. A little superglue goes a long way: you need only one drop per square inch of surface area. Using too much will increase your likelihood of finger-sticking mishaps, increase drying time, and ultimately do a worse job of holding your object together.

15 **Use nail-polish remover to get superglued fingers apart safely.** If your fingers are stuck, do not try to pull them apart. No joke: superglue is so strong that several drops can hold a two-ton truck in the air. Your skin will separate from your finger before it'll break its bond with the glue. Instead, apply a small amount of an acetone-based nail-polish remover on a cotton swab to the glue, and the bond will dissolve. If you don't have any nail-polish remover handy, immerse the bonded skin in warm soapy water, then slowly peel or roll the skin apart. Take your time—you may have to dunk the glued skin in the water several times.

16 **Avoid superglue confusion.** When you're finished using superglue, put it back where it belongs. You don't want to leave the tube someplace where it could be confused for any other product . . . like lip balm! (This might seem unlikely, but it happens so often that physicians created an official term for it: "inadvertent self-administration of superglue.")

17 **Buy fewer, newer batteries.** If your batteries are losing power quickly, you may have bought old ones to start with. If you shop in a store with low turnover, the batteries may have been gathering dust—and losing power—for a while before you came along. This is especially true of closeout and odd-lot stores, where batteries may have sat for a while on the shelf at another store before they even got to yours. Buy only what you need, plus one backup set, and replace your spares when you use them.

18 **Keep batteries out of the fridge.** Batteries don't last any longer when stored in the refrigerator or freezer. In fact, prolonged exposure to extreme cold or heat reduces battery life.

19 **Keep batteries away from metal objects.** When storing batteries, place them so they aren't touching other batteries or anything metal, to be sure they aren't making a connection that will drain them. Don't carry batteries loose in your bag or purse, either; rolling around, they may come into contact with a metal object and lose power.

20 **Remove batteries from unused devices.**
Batteries drain more quickly when they're in an electronic device, even if the device is off. If you have a camera or battery-operated gizmo that you only use from time to time, take the batteries out until you need them. If you have a device that runs on both batteries and electricity, take the batteries out and store them while you're using the wall plug.

21 **Avoid a battery blow-up.** Don't mix new and used, or different types (non-chargeable with rechargeable, for example) of batteries in the same device. When batteries have different levels of charge, the stronger cell will discharge rapidly to compensate for the weaker cell, which can cause it to overheat . . . and, on rare occasions, go boom.

22 **Be extra careful with candles in glass containers.** Remove wax from the previous candle before putting a new candle inside a glass jar. The new candle might tip when the wax underneath it starts to melt, resulting in flame against the glass, which can get hot enough to scald furniture or shatter. The same furnace action can happen if you let a candle burn all the way down. Does the glass container seem thin and chintzy? Cheap glass often can't stand up to the heat. Worse, it can explode after prolonged candle use—sometimes in an unfortunate person's hands.

23 **Cold candles drip less.** To keep candle-wax dripping to a minimum, place tapers in the refrigerator for a few hours before you burn them. As an added bonus, cold candles also last longer!

24 **Check your candle wicks for lead.** If a candle wick contains lead, burning it can spread dangerous amounts of the heavy metal throughout your home. How do you know if your candle has lead in it? You can test it by separating the wick fibers before burning. If you see metal inside, rub the core of the wick on a piece of white paper. If the mark left on the paper is gray, the metallic core is probably lead. Don't burn it!

25 **If it's Baroque, don't fix it.** If you think you may want to sell an antique down the line, don't do anything to fix it up. It might seem like it would be nicer with a fresh coat of paint or a leg that's less wobbly, but in the eyes of an antique collector, that touch-up might reduce its value substantially.

26 **Don't let the news pile up.** If you've planned a long weekend or a vacation, those newspapers piling up on your front porch will give intruders a big, flashy sign that no one's home. Suspend delivery while you're gone, or give a neighborhood kid a few bucks to pick up your papers for you. Keep the focus on your fun getaway, not fears about home.

27 **Dissuade burglars with a few clever devices.** Light timers can create the impression that people are at home. You will better fool would-be burglars if you have two or more lights on timers set to go on and off at different times. You can even buy a device that simulates the glow of a TV and works on a timer. There are also motion-sensitive alarms that play the sound of a barking dog when anyone approaches the house. (A few inexpensive dog toys scattered across the lawn can work as a similar, but quieter, ploy.)

28 **Lock up when you're not home.** A surprising number of burglaries occur with no forced entry. Thieves just walk through unlocked doors and help themselves.

29 **Remember: thieves know about ladders, too.** If you lock the front door and leave the second-floor windows open, your home is not secure. All a thief needs to do is put on a jumpsuit and carry a paintbrush; then they can climb through your window in broad daylight as your neighbor barbecues next door!

30 **Get to know your neighbors.** Besides being the nice thing to do, knowing your neighbors helps with home security. A neighbor you've never met might think that guy wandering around your yard is part of the family. A neighbor who has spent time with you at backyard picnics may just know better and call you or the police. And remember, if you put up a big hedge or fence to wall yourself off from your neighbors, the price of your privacy is that you're providing the same protection for no-goodniks.

31 **Keep out of a break-in.** If you come home and find a broken window, an open door, or other evidence of a break-in, don't go inside. Walk away from the house and call the police.

32 **If you meet a burglar, stay calm.** Most burglars will not attack you; instead, they will simply try to get out of the house as quickly as they can. Try not to do anything that could escalate the situation. Speak in a normal voice, avoid eye contact if possible, and fight only if you are attacked. If you come out with a gun or a baseball bat, the criminal is more likely to become frightened and respond with violence.

LAWN AND GARDEN

1 **Plant the right kind of grass for your lawn.**
If you've got the wrong kind, you may have trouble
maintaining a lush lawn. Traditional bluegrass
has a shallow root structure and can be hard to
keep healthy. Grasses with deeper roots—like
tall fescue or red fescue—require less watering
and are less susceptible to disease. If you already
have bluegrass and don't want to dig it up and
start over, try overseeding it in spring or fall with
another (heartier) bluegrass variety.

2 **Help your lawn take care of itself.** You
shouldn't have to pay a fortune or spray truckloads
of chemical fertilizer to keep your lawn green. A
mower that mulches the grass and leaves it on the
lawn provides natural fertilizer. And you shouldn't

have to weed, either—a thick, healthy lawn will choke out weeds of its own accord!

3 **Check the moisture of your lawn before watering.** To see if your lawn is moist enough, poke it with a stick. It should be moist to a depth of four inches (about ten centimeters). And when it comes to watering your lawn, instead of misting every day, give it a good soak less frequently.

4 **Try a few simple fixes for yellow lawn spots.** Not every yellow spot on your lawn was caused by a pest. Many of these spots just need a little bit of compost. A low spot in your lawn can also turn yellow, especially after a heavy rain. If that's the problem, putting a little soil over the indentation to raise it up to the level of the surrounding ground will fix it.

5 **Water your dog's favorite spots more often.** Yellow patches in your lawn could be caused by the nitrogen in your dog's urine. Even though nitrogen is used in fertilizers, the concentration that is emitted in a dog's urine is too much for grass to take. The way to solve this problem is to dilute the urine after it hits the lawn. Water that spot within eight hours of the deposit to stop yellow circles from forming.

6 **To keep deer out, build a high fence.** If you've already built a fence, but you still see Bambi chomping on your tulips, you didn't make the fence high enough. Deer are excellent jumpers, so to keep them from bounding right in, be sure your fence is at least eight feet high.

7 **Use bar soap to deter deer.** Bar soap can serve the same purpose as chemical deer deterrents, without the nasty odors and toxins. Sprinkle soap shavings on the dirt or dissolve the soap in water and spray it on the plants; either of these will keep deer away. (Just make sure to re-do it after it rains—as with any scent-based deterrents, the rain will wash the soap away!)

8 **You can also repel deer with loud noises.**
Desperate gardeners have had some success
leaving clock radios in the garden, with the
music alarm set to come on slightly after sunset.
Hanging hubcaps or pie tins from cords so they
bang against each other in the wind can also
work—though you might screw up your own sleep
on a windy night.

9 **Guard your plants with plastic mesh.** If you
don't particularly care about what your garden looks
like, covering your plants can keep deer at bay.
(Deer hate sticking their tongues through mesh.)
Upside-down plastic laundry baskets, held securely
in place, will work for shorter individual plants;
lightly wrap plastic netting around taller greens.

10 **Choose plants that deer
don't like.** You can preserve
your yard by cultivating
plants that deer don't like
to eat. They aren't fond
of highly aromatic herbs
like mint, lavender, thyme,
rosemary, and sage. Flowers
that make unpopular deer

snacks include begonias, ageratum, cornflower, marigolds, cleome, and salvia. Deer also tend to steer away from plants with thorns. Ask your local nursery for other suggestions.

11 **Squirrel-proof your bird feeder.** Unless your bird feeder is at least six feet off the ground and ten feet away from trees, squirrels can probably reach it. Once you've chosen the spot you want to hang a feeder, the most effective squirrel deterrent is a baffle. A baffle is a wide plastic disc that fits around the hanging pole. It looks something like a hovering UFO. A squirrel will be able to climb up the pole to the baffle but won't be able to get around it. Alternatively, a dome-shaped baffle above the feeder will keep squirrels from climbing down onto it from above. (And if you don't want to buy a baffle, you can make your own out of anything of a similar shape: a repurposed flowerpot or a section of a two-liter soda bottle should do the trick.)

12 **Give squirrels less helpful materials to grip.** The surface on PVC piping is too slippery for squirrels to get any traction on, so a PVC-mounted bird feeder will be harder for them to climb onto than a pole-mounted one. Hanging bird feeders from wire generally doesn't work—squirrels are impressive aerialists. If you string the line with plastic soda bottles, however, the squirrels will find it harder to traverse.

13 **If raccoons are the real culprits, create bigger barriers.** Raccoons are omnivorous, clever bird-feeder raiders, and they're about ten times the size of your typical squirrel. Keep them out of your feeder using the same techniques you use for squirrels—just be sure that your baffles are wide enough to foil this (much larger) animal.

14 **Use a birdseed mix that squirrels don't like.** Squirrels may gobble down your sunflower seeds, but they're not fond of safflower. They will also turn up their noses at the tiny black nyjer-thistle

seeds that fill tube feeders for finches. Plain white suet—a favorite of woodpeckers—isn't tempting to your rodent nemesis, either.

15 **Good balance prevents bad smells in the compost pile.** If your compost pile smells strong, the problem is most likely either too much moisture or too much nitrogen-rich green material in the pile. Either of these will cause a bad odor. Be sure to balance the mixture properly between green material and brown, carbon-based material such as dead leaves, hay, or straw. Turn the pile regularly to further blend the contents and keep annoying fruit flies and fungus gnats from swarming to it. Keep the compost covered to keep moisture out.

16 **Compost paper, cardboard, and sawdust from untreated wood.** Shred paper first, and break cardboard down into a slurry by ripping it to pieces and adding water. Tissues and paper towels can also be composted without any special treatment. Avoid glossy paper and sawdust from pressure-treated wood. (Pressure-treated wood can leak arsenic into the soil—not ideal for your vegetable garden.)

17 **If gnats are swarming your compost pile, let the top dry out a bit.** Keep your compost bin uncovered long enough to let the top layer of bedding dry out, but make sure that the layers underneath still have the moisture they need. Fungus gnats will stay below the surface where the moisture is, and shouldn't bother you.

18 **Just don't let your compost dry out *too* much.** If your compost pile just sits there and doesn't break down, it may be too dry. In that case, uncover it and let the rain fix the problem. If you're making compost in a warm season, the center of the pile should be warm or even hot to the touch. If it isn't, this is a sign that either the pile is too dry or it's still too small to get a vigorous decomposition going.

19 **Use a banana peel to trick fruit flies out of the house.** Place a banana peel inside a clear plastic container (like a leftover takeout-soup container), and use a toothpick or knife to make three or four holes in the cover, large enough for a fruit fly to crawl through. Put the container near your fruit bowl, indoor compost bin, or wherever fruit flies are congregating. The flies will find

their way in to get to the banana but will not be able to get out. Within twenty-four hours, about 99 percent of the fruit flies in the area will have gotten into the plastic container, at which point you can take the trap outside and let them out.

20 **Dispose of banana peels properly to keep fruit flies away.** Banana peels are one of the most common bearers of fruit-fly larvae. If you're a banana eater and you have a big problem with fruit flies, keep the peels out of the compost and bury them directly in the soil around the plants you want to fertilize. They're a good source of potassium, and are beneficial to flowering plants like roses—but don't bury more than three skins per rosebush per week.

21 **Try a natural mosquito repellant.** For those who prefer to avoid commercial mosquito repellants with DEET or other chemicals, there are a number of natural alternatives. Pennyroyal essential oil, peppermint, vanilla, bay, clove, sassafras, lavender oil, and cedar all have their adherents. Try burning rosemary and sage at your next barbeque—some people swear it keeps mosquitoes at bay. Fresh parsley or apple cider vinegar, rubbed on the skin, are also supposed to be effective. Another popular homemade bug repellant can be concocted with one tablespoon citronella oil, two cups white vinegar, one cup water, and one cup of a base oil to bind it all together, such as grapeseed, almond, or olive oil.

22 **Eliminate standing water outside the house to get rid of mosquitoes.** A mosquito's hunting ground is within about 100 to 200 feet of where she begins her life cycle. (Only egg-bearing females bite people.) Empty out kiddie pools, buckets, and anything else that collects water. If you have a koi pond, keep the water pump in good order. A mosquito that breeds far away from you will bite far away from you, too.

23 **Don't overwater houseplants.** You can recognize an overwatered plant by its yellow leaves, brown leaf tips, and limp appearance. A chronically overwatered plant also begins to shed its leaves. At some point someone might have told you that houseplants should be watered once a week. This is not true! A plant needs water when it's thirsty, and this varies by plant species, season of growth, and relative humidity where the plant lives. The simplest way to determine whether your plant needs water is to touch the soil—if it feels dry, the plant needs water.

24 **Prune overwatered plants to rescue them.** Overwatering a plant causes some of the roots to rot and die. Plants need a direct proportion of root to leaves, so if the roots die, an equal number of leaves need to go. If you bring the root-to-leaf ratio back by pruning in time, the remaining root system will recover enough to take care of the remaining leaves on the plant, eventually creating healthy new roots and foliage.

25 **Use a moisture meter to double-check if your plant needs watering.** Don't leave the meter stuck in the soil all the time—just poke it in when you think the plant might be ready for a drink. Plant experts say to ignore the booklet that comes with the device, about various houseplants and their watering schedules. Let the soil itself give you the information you need.

THE GREAT OUTDOORS

1 **Break in new boots before you hike in them.**
One mistake that new hikers often make is to wait
until a hike to break in a new pair of boots. Break
in your boots early by wearing them around the
house. Try going up and down stairs in them,
and don't forget to see how they feel when you're
carrying your backpack—the extra load can change
how your foot moves inside your shoe. You should
have enough space to wiggle your toes, but not
enough for your foot to slide around.

2 **Avoid cotton socks for hiking.** Cotton socks
retain moisture—one of the main ingredients
for blisters. Instead, get wool hiking socks or
synthetic "moisture-wicking socks." These are
specially designed to keep the moisture off your

feet. If your feet sweat a lot, bring an extra pair on your hike and change socks when they get too damp.

3 **Avoid blisters on a hike by drinking plenty of water.** When your sweat dries, tiny salt crystals remain on your skin and create blister-inducing friction. Keep yourself well hydrated to avoid this.

4 **Wrap with duct tape to prevent blisters.** Many hikers swear by duct tape for avoiding blisters. Wrap the parts of your foot that are blister-prone in the all-purpose tape—it will create a slippery barrier between boot and skin. (And yes, duct tape kept over a wart can remove it, by preventing the wart from breathing. Apparently, the only thing duct tape is *not* good for is sealing ducts!)

5 **Don't try to strike a biting fly where it is.** Instead, anticipate where it might jump and aim a little bit forward of it. A good time to pounce is when the fly has landed and is sitting on a hard surface, rubbing its legs together.

6 **Identify a dangerous snake by its head.** Nonvenomous reptiles—such as your garden-variety garter snake—have long, narrow heads. Almost all venomous snakes in North America—including rattlesnakes, copperheads, and water moccasins—are pit vipers, which have wide, triangle-shaped heads. Pit vipers also have long hollow fangs, and use "pits" on the sides of their heads (hence the name) to sense the presence of warm-blooded creatures that they hope will make good snacks.

7 **Whether a snake is venomous or not, give it a wide berth.** Even nonvenomous snakes will strike if they feel threatened.

8 **Move away from a snake—but don't overdo it.** Snakes can only strike up to a distance of about half their own length. Leave most snakes alone, and they'll slither away on their own. If you feel that you must remove a snake from your yard, spray it gently with a garden hose while keeping your distance.

9 **Never pick up a dead snake.** It may not be quite dead yet.

10 **See a doctor right away if you are bitten by a snake.** Even if you are absolutely certain it's not venomous, you should see a doctor. The bite may not kill or injure you right away, but many snakes carry germs that can lead to serious illness or infection if the wounds are left untreated.

11 **Keep your bearings while hiking.** Be sure to check your compass and look for landmarks periodically whenever you're on a hike. Then, when you're tracking back, you'll know that the big rock where you saw the frog was due east of the purple wildflowers, which were growing near the path that leads to the place where you parked your car.

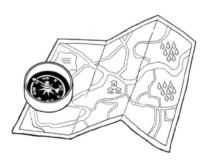

12 **Don't rely entirely on a compass to get you home.** Keep a map in your backpack, so if you do stumble onto a roadway, you can pull it out and figure out exactly where you are.

13 **Make your own daytime compass.** If there's enough sunlight to cast a shadow, you can make a sun compass to help you find your bearings. Find three big sticks, and drive one into the ground in an open area. Then lay another stick on the ground to mark the line of its shadow, all the way up to the end. Wait about fifteen minutes until the line moves, then mark the new line with the last stick, with its end lined up with the end of the shadow. Now draw a line between the ends of these two sticks (or, if you've run out of sticks, you can use your finger). You now have an east-to-west guideline! You can take additional bearings in the same way over further 15-minute increments, if you'd like to be sure your line is correct.

14 **Color-code tent joints for easy assembly.** When buying a new tent, buy a set of colored paints or masking tape along with it. Use these different colors to mark the various joints of your new tent. This kind of color-coding will be much easier to follow than a set of soggy instructions.

15 **Keep track of all of your tent pieces.** Tie the various components of your tent directly to the tent body. If you know you're prone to losing things, order some extra fly poles and connecters now. While you're at it, spare yourself any unpleasant surprises by packing duct tape, a nylon patch kit, and a coil of parachute cord along with your tent.

16 **Set up a new tent at home before you take it camping.** Do it in your backyard or living room when you aren't wet, hungry, or tired. Be sure you understand all the pieces so you don't end up stuffing something back in the bag, only to realize

later (perhaps when you wake up soaking wet) how important it was.

17 **Pitch your tent on level ground.** This will keep you from getting soaked from the ground up. Even small depressions will fill with water when it rains. If the ground is wet to begin with, put down a tarp first and pitch your tent on top of that.

18 **Thoroughly clear the ground beneath your tent.** Unless you like sleeping with hard things poking into your back, remove as many rocks and branches as you can. Of course, you'll also want to steer clear of anthills, poison ivy, and suspicious holes that could be small animals' burrows. For a little extra comfort, pile dead grass or pine boughs underneath the tent—it will provide you with a softer bed and keep you warmer, as you'll have less direct contact with the ground.

19 **Pitch your tent in the right direction.** If possible, pitch your tent facing east or southeast. That way you'll get to enjoy the sun's morning rays, as well as shade in the afternoon.

20 **Stake down your tent.** To avoid turning your tent into a giant windsail, pin down the corners with tent stakes. If you're trying to put up your tent on soil that's too sandy for stakes, you can bury a log and use it as a base for the stake instead.

21 **Don't turn your tent into a smokehouse—or a fire hazard.** Your campfire should be upwind of your tent, at least ten to fifteen feet away. Even "fireproof" tents will ignite if a big enough spark lands on them!

22 **Purify your own drinking water.** If you're roughing it, you don't always want to have to lug a heavy water bottle into the woods along with all your other gear. Fortunately, it doesn't take a great deal of effort to make most water safe for drinking: all you have to do is bring it to a good rolling boil. (Many guides suggest that you keep the water boiling for twenty minutes, but this isn't necessary, and wastes fuel.)

23 **Pack an easy, reliable fire-starter.** A lighter is much more consistent than matches.

24 **Clear a ten-foot safety zone around your fire.** To keep from starting a forest fire, it's important to choose a good spot for your blaze. You'll need a clearing far away from houses, trees, dangling branches, your neighbor's tent, and so on. A clear area of at least ten feet (about three meters) in diameter is a good rule of thumb.

25 **Wall in your fire with rocks.** Create a perimeter of rocks about three or four feet (one meter) around the center of the place where you plan to build your fire. This will keep the fire contained, should it escape the pit. Remember that sparks can rise on the air and land a good distance from your fire, so if conditions are especially dry, don't build a campfire. Dry grass can burn in all directions much faster than you think—and can quickly get out of control.

26 **Use light but durable kindling.** To get the fire going, kindling has to burn long enough and hot enough. Lightweight materials such as old papers make good kindling. If you're out in nature without a stack of old bills or newspapers, look for some of these standbys: birch or cedar bark, dry grass and leaves, dry moss, dead evergreen needles, and down from milkweed, pussy willows, or cattails.

27 **Build your fire in a pyramid.** Small sticks and branches for the campfire should be broken up and placed around the kindling in a pyramid shape. It's best to use resinous softwoods, such as pine, to get the fire going, then switch to hardwoods for the long haul. Softwoods are smoky and throw sparks, but they light quickly. Hardwoods take longer to ignite, but they provide a steady heat and burn down into satisfying embers.

28 **Be sure your fire is completely out when you leave.** Drench the fire with as much water as you can, then throw dirt on the coals. Just be sure the dirt doesn't contain any small twigs and leaves, which can be ignited by hot coals hours after you think the fire has gone out. Before you leave your campsite, hold your hand over the pit. If you can't feel any heat, you're free to go.

29 **Wear your life vest while out on a boat.**
One professional fisherman's recent drowning
in Scotland was widely attributed to the culture
on the vessel, which made him "feel a sissy" for
wearing a life saver. Life jackets are orange, they're
puffy, they're not the least bit fashion-forward . . .
and they can save your life.

30 **While fishing, wear boots with non-skid
soles.** Your boots should be at least one size
larger than your normal street shoes. That way,
you can wear extra socks inside to keep your feet
warm. Also, if you do get pulled overboard, you
can kick them off easily and swim.

31 **Don't underestimate the fight in a fish.**
Fishermen have somehow not acquired a
reputation for daring adventure. Yet they're
performing essentially the same task as a
toreador—they're fighting an animal to its death.
If a fisherman or his friend gets caught in the line,
the force of a thrashing fish engaged in a life-and-
death struggle can be surprisingly strong.

32 **Stay alert to avoid stray hooks.** Most fishing
injuries are caused by humans, not fish. The

sharp, barbed hooks that fishermen use to pierce fish flesh do just as well with the human kind. A fisherman needs to pay careful attention when he casts his line so he doesn't catch something on his backswing—himself or his fishing buddy, for example.

33 **Protect your eyes while fishing.** Sunglasses are a good choice: not only do they protect your eyes from UV rays, but they also reduce your risk of getting a hook in the eye. If a hook does get into someone's eye, have the victim look straight ahead with both eyes closed. (If one eye stays open and is tempted to move, the other eye will mirror its movements.) Immobilize the lure with cloth strips or tape, or by placing a cup over the lure

and taping it in place. Then get to the hospital as quickly as you can.

34 **Carry wire cutters to fix a fish hook snafu.** If a hook does get into your skin, cut the barb off and remove it if it's not too deep. Clean and dress the wound. If the barb is deeply embedded, or if it's in a sensitive spot like the face, head, or neck, do *not* try to unhook it yourself. Get the injured person to a trained physician as quickly as possible.

35 **Snap a snagged fishing line efficiently.** If your line gets snagged beneath the surface of moving water, let the line spool out downstream. This may change the angle of resistance. If you do need to break the line off, reduce the tension, point the rod directly at the snag, turn your back, and walk away until the line snaps.

36 **Never, ever run from a bear.** Bears can run much faster than you. If you encounter a bear, don't panic or behave aggressively, because this may further upset her. Back away from the bear while speaking in a soothing voice.

COLD WEATHER

1 **Fidget more to keep warm.** Shivering is the body's natural way of urging you to warm up by moving. Movement burns calories, which creates heat, so if you're caught in the cold, even little actions like stamping your feet can help.

2 **Know your body's hot spots.** Tucking your hands under your arms can ward off frostbite in your fingers—there are major arteries in your armpits that carry warm blood from your heart. (A similar junction can be found in your groin, but tucking your hands there is not always socially practical.)

3 **Keep your head covered in the cold, but don't overdo it.** It's a myth that you lose most of your body's heat through your head. It is, of course, important to protect your head and ears on a cold day, and keeping your head warm can cue the rest of your body to preserve heat, too—but only 8 to 10 percent of your body's heat emanates from your head. If you're buried up to your neck in snow, a good hat won't do much to keep you warm!

4 **Dressing in layers can generate warmth.** Layering isn't just about a flexible wardrobe; it can actually keep you warmer than a single thick sweater. Your body heat, trapped in the air between layers of clothing, delivers bonus warmth. For the best impact, choose an outer layer that serves as a waterproof armor over a softer, insulated layer, followed by a layer against the skin that evaporates sweat and other moisture quickly.

5 **When walking on ice, just relax.** Bend your knees a bit, and lean slightly forward. That way, even if you do miscalculate and fall, you'll go down forward—which is far less dangerous than falling backward. A shuffle beats a normal step. Inch your way forward, taking tiny steps. If you're still having trouble walking on the ice, turn sideways and shuffle along that way. If all else fails, sit down and slide along on your butt.

6 **Take a tip from your kids on how to fall without getting hurt.** Have you ever noticed how kids seem to be able to come crashing down only to stand right back up, giggling? That's because when they fall, they tense their muscles less than adults do. Try to keep relaxed through a fall, and you may be able to come up laughing, too.

7 **When tying ice skates, make them snug on the bottom but loose on top.** You want your ankle to be well supported, but the top of the boot shouldn't be so rigid that you can't bend your foot. Don't forget to keep the tongue in the correct position: in the middle of the opening between the sides of the boot. Keep it flat and in place as you lace up your skates. When you've finished lacing, try to bend your ankle so your knees are over your toes. If you can't do it, the top is too tight—sit down, unlace them, and try again.

8 **Falling while skating is normal.** It's inevitable that a beginning skater will fall at least once, so just relax and don't be embarrassed! It's part of the learning process.

Being relaxed is one of the keys to skating well. Besides, it'll also hurt more if your muscles are tense when you hit the ice!

9 **Keep moving while skating.** Believe it or not, falls taken at speed are usually less painful than the tumbles you have while standing still! Try to land on your side when you go down, and get up quickly so other skaters don't trip over you.

10 **Practice stopping on the ice.** Before you get skating too fast, remember that you will eventually have to stop. To do so, bend your knees slightly and push your feet outward, leading with the heels and letting your toes move apart.

11 **Survive falling through ice by staying calm.** When you plunge into the cold, the shock will cause you to gasp for air and start hyperventilating. If you don't control your breathing, you may inhale freezing water—so stay calm and get to the surface. Once you have your breathing under control, you have about ten minutes to swim to safety before your muscle and nerve fibers become too cold to function properly. (This is one area where being overweight is an advantage: if you have extra body fat, you'll survive a bit longer in the cold.) If you can't get out of the water and are running out of time, try to freeze your arms to the ice to keep yourself from sinking when you lose consciousness.

12 **Use salt water to simplify scraping your car windows.** Before a snowstorm, wipe your windows with a sponge dipped in salt water, then let them dry. The salt will discourage ice formation on the windows during the storm. The next time you go out to your car, the windows shouldn't be coated with ice.

13 **Don't scrape your car while the car's still cold.** Start up the car, and let it warm up with the defroster running. While it's warming up, go back into the house and whip up some homemade de-icer. A number of combinations will work for this. Try a mixture of one cup water, one cup rubbing alcohol, and one cup vinegar, or use 50 percent water and 50 percent ethyl alcohol, or 50 percent water and 50 percent vinegar. Pour one of these solutions—or just salt—over the windshield, and wait a minute or two for it to work before scraping. You may barely need to scrape at all!

14 **Apply chemical de-icer only to windows.**
Chemical de-icer is corrosive, and if you get it on your car's paint, it can eat away at that sweet cherry finish. Make sure you have plenty of windshield washer fluid in the reservoir, and carry an extra gallon with you during cold months—road salt is great for keeping roads ice-free, but it coats everything.

15 **If you're caught in a blizzard while driving, pull over.** You may be tempted to try toughing out the blizzard, but hurtling in a steel box over icy roads, even at slow speeds, is a terrible idea. If you're blinded by a whiteout, pull over and put on your hazard lights so other cars can see you. If you have a cell phone, call emergency services. Unless you can see a building very close to you, don't get out and walk for help—you can easily get turned around and lost in a whiteout. Police and rescue vehicles are far more likely to find you and come to your aid if you're in your car.

16 **If you're stopped in a blizzard, limit the time you spend running the heater in your car.**
Keep yourself warm, but only run the heater for about ten minutes each hour. Any longer, and

you risk running out of gas or filling the car with carbon monoxide gas. If the snow is heavy, go out occasionally and check to be sure that the exhaust pipe is free of snow—if it's blocked at all, carbon monoxide can seep into the car. (And if it's blocked entirely, the car won't start.)

17 **Watch for slow-to-show health problems after exposure to cold.** Don't assume that you weren't harmed by the cold just because the effects weren't immediate. Many winter deaths aren't caused by hypothermia. Extreme cold strains the body, weakens the immune system, and causes a series of changes in the blood. These changes increase the chances of blood clots forming, which can lead to heart attacks and strokes a day or two after exposure.

18 **Never rub a frostbitten area with snow.** Where this myth began is a mystery, but the last thing you want to do with frozen skin is chill it further. Instead, bring the area back to normal temperature slowly by immersing it in warm—never hot—water. Frostbitten skin cannot feel pain, and if the water is too hot, you might burn yourself without knowing it.

19

Don't assume a hot drink will warm you up.
Hot drinks like coffee and cocoa are pleasing on cold days, but the effect is more psychological than physical. If you want a drink to really keep you warm, drink anything—cold or hot—with a lot of sugar in it. Sugar gives you a burst of warming calories.

TRAVEL AND LEISURE

1 **When giving directions, limit your information.** You only want to give whatever information will truly help the person you're directing. If you list everything a driver is likely to pass along a route, nothing will stick! Limit your landmarks to things that help tell a driver where to turn, when to start looking for an intersection, or where to stop. Here's the right way to do it: "Pull out of the parking lot here and turn right. Drive three blocks and you will come to Main Street. *You'll recognize it because you'll see a big high school on the right."*

2 **When giving directions over the phone, orient yourself properly.** If the person you're directing is at a gas station or a fast-food restaurant, remember that these often have entrances on more than one street. Be sure you know which way the caller is oriented before saying something like "pull out of the parking lot and turn right"—you might be visualizing different streets. Instead say, "Pull out on Rochester Road and turn right."

3 **Tailor your directions to your listener.** Remember, different people process the information in directions differently. Some people like a route perspective, which focuses on turns and landmarks from the point of view of the traveler. Others are more comfortable with a spatial perspective, with directions like east and west as they appear on a map. You can help most travelers by offering a bit of both.

4 **Travel with a guidebook or multi-language dictionary.** These are especially useful in foreign restaurants, where they'll allow you to communicate a few key ingredients by pointing to them in the book. You can also download translation apps for your phone, some of which will even speak for you.

5 **Learn a few phrases in the local language.**
It always pays to learn a few key phrases when
you travel. If there are certain foods you want to
avoid—if you have an allergy, for example, or if you
simply have no desire to try a poodle steak—those
are some of the first words you should learn.

6 **Start "living" the time zone at your
destination before you get there.** To avoid
jet lag, try to sleep—or stay awake—and eat as
though you were already where you're going. If
it's daytime in your destination, try to stay awake.
If it is nighttime there, try to sleep. Airline meals
are usually served based on the time zone you're
leaving, so bring your own snacks or wait until a
time that's appropriate to your destination time
zone to eat the meal they give you.

LONDON   NEW YORK   TOKYO   MOSCOW

7 **For larger time-zone changes, try "phase-shifting" your meal times.** In preparation for a trip that will take you across multiple time zones, start eating in keeping with your destination time zone over the course of a week before you depart. This can reduce the shock to your system. If you can, arrive a day before your planned activities to give yourself time to adjust.

8 **Avoid stomach distress while traveling abroad by drinking soda.** Besides being sterile, bottled drinks such as cola are usually somewhat acidic, making your stomach an inhospitable environment for microbes. Just be sure to order your drink without ice—ice is, of course, frozen local water, and can make you sick if you're not used to whatever bacteria happens to be in it.

9 **Drink bottled water while traveling.** Tap water in foreign countries can wreak havoc on your stomach. (You'll also want to keep some bottled water in your hotel room for brushing your teeth.) In foreign restaurants, consider politely asking for bottled water to be opened in front of you. If your water bottle comes out sans cap, it may just be tap water in a bottle.

10 **Play it safe with raw and fresh foods while traveling.** Most travelers' intestinal maladies derive not from contaminated water but from poor food-handling practices. Harmful microbes that are introduced to food breed quickly, posing a greater risk than water alone. When in doubt, avoid fresh salad fixings and vegetables washed in local water, or raw fruits that you haven't peeled yourself. If you can, eat in places where you can directly watch the food being prepared.

11 **Treat gambling as fun, not business.** Playing the slots is not a retirement plan or a way to get out of a financial bind. It's a form of entertainment. Think of a gambling outing as a trip to a ballgame or an amusement park—these outings can cost a lot of money, but if you plan ahead and choose an event you can afford, you'll enjoy the memory of a fun experience afterward, whether you win or lose.

12 **Set a gambling budget.** That way, if you spend all of it, it's fine. If you have a tendency to think,

Oh, just another twenty bucks can't hurt, then only take as much cash with you as you're willing to lose, and leave your cards at home or in the hotel room. That way, you can't overspend—no matter how much all those free cocktails may make you want to.

13 Know how much money you'll need for an evening of slots. It costs about $9 an hour to play a nickel machine with a three-coin maximum. A quarter machine will cost about $45 an hour, and a dollar machine will cost $180 an hour.

14 Follow the 1 percent rule while gambling. Don't make bets higher than 1 percent of your budget. If you're ahead, you can raise your bets a bit—but never chase after money you've lost. Take a deep breath and walk away. You should also walk away if you find you're ahead. If you win $100 and

then lose $20, quit while you're ahead, use your winnings on a relaxing dinner, and then move to another table for a new game if you still want to play.

15 **Enjoy the show at big casinos—but gamble at the smaller ones.** If you're visiting the Strip, visit the theme casinos for the shows and ambiance, but do your gaming at the smaller casinos a bit off the main tourist path. The big casinos have a steady stream of tourists and don't need to offer the best odds.

16 **Learn to spot marked cards.** You can check to see if cards have been marked by riffling the deck and watching the design on the back. If the deck has been marked, the design will move like an animated flip-book.

17 **Check for loaded dice.** You can spot a loaded die by dropping it into a tall glass of water. Do this several times with different numbers on top—if the dice turn while sinking, allowing the same two or three numbers to always show up, the dice are loaded. (If it would be a bit too conspicuous to do this in the middle of a casino, hold the die lightly between your thumb and forefinger by diagonally opposite corners. A loaded die will pivot when the weighted side is on top.)

18 **Never buy more than one lottery ticket at a time.** Think of it like this: With one ticket, you have one opportunity to imagine being filthy rich. If you buy five tickets, your odds of winning don't go up that much, and you're still only getting one chance to dream.

19 **To raise your odds of a big lottery payoff, play unpopular numbers.** This will not actually increase your odds of winning, but if you do win, it may increase the amount, because you'll split it with fewer winners. Unpopular numbers include anything over 31. (This is because many people choose their birth dates or anniversaries, and no one was born or married on the 32nd.) After

that, choose numbers ending in 1, 2, 8, 9, and 0. Most people, for whatever reason, tend to select numbers ending in 3 through 7.

20 **Know the limitations on a quick-pick ticket.** If you buy a quick-pick ticket, there's a chance that you could match all of the numbers without actually winning the prize! Under the rules of most state lotteries, only a certain number of quick-pick tickets can hit the jackpot in a single game. If more than that are printed, the lottery commission can disqualify all of them.

21 **Enter sweepstakes instead of playing the lottery.** Sweepstakes cost nothing to enter, and they still give you the chance to imagine being the winner of exotic vacations, new cars, and piles of cash. And if you enter enough of them, you'll probably win the occasional consolation prize, which is a nice little pick-me-up!

FUN AND GAMES

1 **Rule number one of Rock, Paper, Scissors: Rock is for rookies.** Inexperienced players tend to open with Rock, so if you throw Paper against one, you usually win. If you're playing with a pro who knows the "Rock is for rookies" rule, try throwing Scissors. Your opponent will either open with Paper or Scissors, so you'll either cut his Paper or tie his Scissors.

2 **People hate being predictable—even in Rock, Paper, Scissors.** They will almost never throw the same thing three times in a row. You can use this to your advantage. If your opponent throws Paper twice, his next move is almost guaranteed to be something else. That leaves only two options: Scissors or Rock. Throw Rock: you'll either smash his Scissors or tie his Rock. Another psychological tip: If your Rock, Paper, Scissors opponent has lost the last round, he will often come back by throwing the move that would have beaten the last round. For example, if you smashed his Scissors with your Rock, he will likely throw Paper on the next move.

3 **Try a little mind control to win at Rock, Paper, Scissors.** If you have trouble outthinking your opponent at the breakneck speed of Rock, Paper, Scissors game play, prime your opponent to throw what you would like him to. When you bring up the idea of playing the game, keep making a gesture for the move you want your opponent to play. The other player will often subconsciously accept your nonverbal suggestion.

4 **Learn the right words to win at Scrabble.** Two-letter words should be your first priority. Not only do the "twos" help you fit into tight corners, but they also help you line up parallel plays, where you form two or more words along two axes. The National Scrabble Association says learning the twos will increase your scoring by an average of thirty to forty points a game. Next, you will want to learn the twenty-one legal words beginning with "Q" that don't need a "U" after it. Believe it or not, the typewriter word "qwerty" counts, as does "qi" (the circulating life energy in Chinese philosophy).

5 **Be strategic with the letters in your Scrabble rack.** The least-valuable letters in terms of scoring and playability are Q, V, W, B, F, O, and P. Try to get rid of them as quickly as you can, but hold onto S, E, R, D, and Y. These are useful as "hooks": you can use them to turn someone's "twerp" into "twerps" and build a whole new word with the S. The ideal Scrabble-letter ratio is four consonants to three vowels; the only duplicate letters worth keeping are E and O (O is better in pairs than on its own). Look for any letters that form prefixes (like "pre-") or suffixes (like "-ed") and set those to one side.

6 **Keep track of already-played Scrabble letters.** Top Scrabble players use tracking sheets to keep track of all of the letters that have been played. This gives them an idea of what letters are left in the bag and on their opponent's rack. You might also want to write down all of the tiles on your rack on each turn, so you can see later what words you missed. This will help you improve.

7 **Use a pencil on crossword puzzles.** Everyone makes mistakes, and those boxes are too small to accommodate ballpoint pen cross-outs. The harder puzzles—especially the ones that torment you on Sundays—sometimes have multiple answers that fit, but only one that works with the other answers.

8 **Don't go through crossword clues in order.** Instead of solving, for example, all of the acrosses and then all of the downs, work outward from your first completed word. It will be easier to find right answers quickly if you have at least one letter to help you.

9 **Start with the fill-in-the-blank crossword clues.** These are generally among the easiest crossword clues to solve, so scan the list and start with those. Next, concentrate on the short answers. Once you've taken up the crossword habit, you will start to notice familiar words that tend to creep in. Puzzle makers need words that begin and end with vowels, so you're likely to come across *epee*, *aloe*, *Arlo*, *anoa*, *esne*, and similar words in your crossword travels. The more puzzles you do, the more freebies like this you'll discover.

10 **As you fill in a crossword puzzle, try to get an idea of its theme.** Not all crossword puzzles have themes, but most do. Figuring out the theme will help you with the long words. The long answers are likely to be multiple-word phrases involving some sort of wordplay; these are also the likeliest to represent the puzzle's theme.

11 **Pay attention to the wording of crossword clues.** These will give you some idea as to the form of the answer. For example, if the clue contains a foreign word, the answer is likely to be in a foreign language. If the clue contains an abbreviation, the answer probably does, too. If the clue is plural, ends in -*ing*, or is in the past tense, the answer should follow that pattern.

12 **When interpreting a crossword clue, look past the most obvious read.** Some words—such as golf and love—can be read as a noun, a verb, or an adjective. Some clues are cryptic: For example, "She meets him halfway across the living room" seems like nonsense at first, but if you look halfway across "living room," you'll see "groom."

13 **Don't get locked into one meaning with crossword clues.** If you're stuck, go back and reconsider the answers you've already filled in. One of them might be wrong.

14 **Be systematic when you carve a pumpkin.** The big mistake that most pumpkin novices make is to start by cutting off the top and hollowing out the inside before they even start to put on a face. Instead, try keeping the top attached and wait until you're done carving the design to hollow out the inside. You'll have more control cutting into a solid pumpkin, and if the stem is attached, you'll have something to grab onto.

15 **Use a small, sharp knife to carve pumpkins.** Not only are big chef's knives hard to maneuver, they require more force, which makes them more dangerous. With a small knife and a vegetable peeler, you can produce a wide variety of effects. Start by stripping off the outer orange flesh from one side of the pumpkin to create a soft canvas that's easy to carve and that gives off a glow when lit.

16 **Start your pumpkin carving with a stencil or drawing.** Pictures from children's coloring books work well for designs. Remember that straight lines are easier to cut into a pumpkin than curved ones. Tape your picture on, then use the tip of a sharp pencil to make a dotted line around the lines of the image. This line of dots will be transferred onto the pumpkin. Then you can slice along your dotted line.

17 **Repair pumpkin-carving mistakes.** If you cut off a piece that you didn't mean to, don't worry—it's repairable. Grab some toothpicks and use them to tack the piece back onto the pumpkin. You can also use staples that you push in with your hand. Depending on the image, this could make your jack-o'-lantern even scarier!

18 **Wash and dry your carved pumpkin to make it last longer.** Once you've finished carving your pumpkin and cleaning out the pulp and seeds, wash and rinse your creation inside and out, then dry it thoroughly. A clean, dry pumpkin will last longer. A thin coat of petroleum jelly on its cut surfaces will also extend your jack-o'-lantern's life.

19 **Keep your pumpkin-carving space clean.** Unless you want to clean up orange pulp for days, it's best to carve pumpkins outside, or lay down newspapers where you'll be working. Keep some towels nearby to wipe your hands of pumpkin guts at regular intervals. Working with clean hands is not only more pleasant, but it'll also keep your knife from slipping.

20 **The secret to find a good boomerang.** Many of the boomerangs you find at toy stores will never come back, no matter how great your technique may be. They just don't have the right design. Steer away from flexible plastic boomerangs, too—these don't hold their shape, so the best you can hope for is that they will curve slightly before falling out of the sky. You want a boomerang with arms shaped like airplane wings—curved on one side, flat on the other.

21 **Don't throw a boomerang like a Frisbee.** A boomerang is flat, not round like a baseball, so you may be tempted to throw it as if it were a disc. This is the wrong way to throw it, and it could set up a dangerous flight pattern. Instead, hold the boomerang by one tip, with your thumb on the rounded side. The boomerang should curve so the top wing points forward. Aim at a spot slightly above the horizon, and throw with a smooth, hard motion. Snap your hand at a slight angle, about 65 degrees to the horizon. As it completes its turn, it will start spinning horizontally and much more slowly. This is the time to trap it: Clap your hands together from above and below the boomerang, keeping your body to the side of the flight path. If you miss, you don't want to be slapped in the face by a big wooden stick!

22 **Turn Frisbee into a team sport.** After a few tosses, your kids might become bored with their new Frisbee. Take the game to new heights by setting up a disc golf range in the backyard or local park: designate starting points and ending points just like in a game of golf, and see who can get there in the fewest tosses. Alternatively, set up a game of Ultimate Frisbee by dividing the group into two teams who try to pass the frisbee to their end zone, with no player keeping the Frisbee for longer than ten seconds.

IN THE AIR

1 **Pack light.** A good rule of thumb: if you have to sit on your bag to close it, you're probably taking too much stuff. There are good reasons to pack light. Not only do airlines charge you for checked or overweight bags, but lugging heavy bags are also a leading cause of injury among travelers.

2 **Don't pack every piece of clothing you like.** Bring enough clean underwear for every day of your journey, unless it's very long and you'll have the chance to do laundry. For outerwear, just choose a few items that can go from day to night. Pick neutral colors so that you can mix and match a few key pieces to make different outfits. Clothing made of synthetic fabrics is less prone to wrinkling and tends to be lighter than clothing made of natural fabrics, making it a good travel option. (And if you think you might need to do some hand-washing on your journey, these fabrics will also usually dry more quickly.)

3 **Roll, don't fold, your packed clothes.** The biggest mistake amateur packers make is folding clothing to keep it wrinkle-free. You want to do just the opposite. Roll everything from socks to suits. Rolled clothing does not move around as much in the suitcase, which is what causes clothes to wrinkle. What's more, rolling allows you to fit more clothing into a smaller bag.

4 **Know the TSA rules for liquids.** If you're traveling by air, Transportation Security Administration (TSA) regulations allow only a small amount of liquid to be brought onto a flight in your carry-on. Remember the 3-1-1 rule: You're allowed to carry liquid and gels only in 3.4-ounce bottles or smaller, all of which must be packed in a 1-quart, clear, plastic, zip-top bag. Each passenger is allowed one such bag. Keep this on top of the other stuff in your carry-on—you'll likely have to take it out and put it in the screening bin. (This may seem like a hassle, but it actually helps you pack more lightly.)

5 **Choose a seat assignment when you book your flight.** This gives you the best chance of avoiding the dreaded middle seat. Never wait until you arrive at the airport to pick your seat, if you can help it. When booking online, try to choose a seat in a row that's three across, in which only one seat is already reserved. The middle seat between two people traveling alone is least likely to fill up, so if the flight isn't too full, you may get some extra breathing room.

6 **If your seat is switched to one you don't like, try to switch it again.** Even if you choose a seat while booking online, the airline might just "reclaim" your seat for favored customers— so be sure to check in at the airport an hour or more before departure. If you find you're in a seat you don't like, go to the airline's desk as soon as someone shows up there and see if you can get a seat change. (That's when all the reserved seats of no-show passengers are released.)

7 **Keep off-color jokes to yourself while flying.** If you've got a really funny joke that involves bombs, guns, and planes, save it for when you're out of the airport—and don't post travel-security jokes on your social media stream, either. Airport security officers are trained to take any verbal threats seriously, and have been known to put people in jail for statements that were intended as jests.

8 **Try not to complain about security, either.** If you annoy airport security enough, they have the right to take you out of the line and put you through the highest level of scrutiny. This could delay you enough to miss your flight.

9 **Don't hesitate while walking through a metal detector.** Walk through metal detectors in one brisk stride. If you stop halfway or brush up against the side of the detector, you can cause a first alarm—and if you set it off, you only get one more try before you're subject to a full search.

10 **In a full-body scanner, follow the diagram.**
You need to assume the position on the diagram
and hold still. Putting your hands over your head
and spreading your legs may make you feel like a
bit of a criminal, but it's easier to grin and bear this
than to make a fuss and potentially miss your flight.

11 **Drink plenty of liquids on your flight.** Jet lag
is exacerbated by dehydration, which many people
experience during a flight. Drink plenty
of liquids, and try to avoid alcohol and
coffee. If you eat carbohydrates before
bed when you arrive, it will help you go to
sleep and be loaded up for the next day.
Then eat a high-protein breakfast on the
first day in your new destination—the
protein will help you stay awake and
energized through that first day.

12 **Don't reach for the melatonin when you
travel.** Recent studies have found no evidence
that melatonin tablets are effective in preventing
jet lag. You may get a small placebo effect—but
this should just show you how important your
perception can be. If you don't *think* you'll be jet-
lagged, you will probably feel less jet-lagged.

13 **Pick the right seat to minimize motion sickness when you fly.** Choose a seat over the wing on the right side of the plane to minimize motion sickness. Most flight patterns turn left, so you won't be jostled around as much if you sit on the right.

14 **Increase your odds of surviving a plane crash.** There's one simple thing you can do to increase your odds of survival: follow the emergency directions. Listening to the safety instructions at the beginning of your flight, and actually reading the emergency pamphlet the airline provides for you, can actually save your life.

15 **Get away from a crashed plane as quickly as possible.** After a plane crashes, you have only ninety seconds to get out before fire can cause the cabin temperature to rise to more than 2000°F. This will usually start a so-called flashover fire, which is the combustion of everything around due to that insane level of heat. Again, you'll be less likely to give in to negative panic if you've mentally rehearsed the steps from the safety instructions before an emergency happens.

16 **Pay no attention to advice on selecting airline seats to survive an accident.** Every crash is different, which means that different parts of the plane will be impacted. There are no particularly accident-proof seats. Focus more on keeping calm—if you can reduce your anxiety level, you'll be safer. (After all, your risk of dying from a stress-induced heart attack in the airport is much greater than your chance of dying in a plane crash!)

17 **Don't worry too much about turbulence while flying.** Turbulence is uncomfortable and might give you air sickness, but it's not going to take down the plane. If flying makes you nervous and you'd like to avoid a bumpy ride, schedule your flight for the morning, when thunderstorms are less likely. Also, try to sit toward the front of the plane—you'll feel the turbulence a bit less there than in the back.

ON THE ROAD

1 **Lock up your bike.** Many bikes are stolen each year simply because people fail to lock them up. And this isn't quite as negligent as it may seem at first—most unlocked bikes are stolen out of people's yards or off their porches.

2 **Watch out for a bike thief's favorite spots.** Bike thieves like to do their shopping where they're most likely to find lots of poorly locked cycles: college campuses are popular targets, for example. Exercise special caution in these areas.

3 **Lock your bike to something that can't be taken away.** If you lock your bike to a wobbly pole, someone can lift the pole out of the ground and slide your lock right off of it. Don't lock

your bicycle to parking meters or anything that is posted as illegal, either, or your bike may be "stolen" by the cops!

4 **Don't use wimpy bike locks.** That chain bike lock you used when you were a kid is not enough to thwart a modern thief. The best choice is usually a good U-lock for the back tire and frame, combined with a cable lock for the front tire. Put the U of the U-lock through the back tire and frame and around the pole you're locking it to. Run the cable lock through the front tire and through the U-Lock, and then lock the U-Lock.

5 **Don't leave items attached to your bike when you're locking up.** If you leave your water bottle and backpack on your bike, they might not be there when you come back. Be sure to take everything with you that you want to keep.

6 **Learn to drive a manual transmission car.** A standard transmission car gets better gas mileage and, if you drive it right, will extend the life of your brakes. Car shopping will be less painful, too, as springing for a manual transmission can cut a car's price by $800 to $1,200. It's also less likely to be stolen—newspaper archives are full of accounts of would-be thieves who were thwarted because they didn't know how to drive a stick shift!

7 **Keep your car tuned up.** A car that's tuned up and in proper running condition will have better gas mileage. Change your oil, oil filter, air filter, and spark plugs according to the schedule in your car's service manual.

8 **Keep your tires inflated.** A properly inflated tire rolls more easily than a flat one. If the car runs more easily, it uses less energy, which saves gas.

9 **If your "Check Engine" light comes on, don't ignore it.** It could mean that the vehicle's oxygen sensor has failed, which could reduce your car's fuel efficiency by much as 40 percent.

10 **Save fuel by dropping heavy loads sooner rather than later.** The heavier the car, the more energy it takes to move it down the road. If your SUV is always loaded up with sporting equipment and broken appliances you meant to take to the recycling center, you're spending a bit more than you would if it were empty.

11 **Don't drive too aggressively.** Not only is it rude, but it burns up a lot of fuel. You'll get the best gas mileage if you can keep a consistent gas-pedal position. (This is why highway driving is more fuel efficient than stop-and-go city driving.) Let off the gas pedal early, and ease onto the brakes when you're coming to a stop. When you start moving, go easy on the gas and accelerate slowly.

12 **Don't leave unnecessary devices running in your car.** Any device in the car that uses energy—headlights, defroster, automatic seat warmers, air conditioner—reduces your gas mileage by some amount. Leaving the rear defroster on the entire time you're driving, well after the window is frost-free, can make a difference at the pump.

13 **Don't run your car's air conditioner more than you have to.** It can be a big drain on your tank. Here's the catch, though: If you're traveling more than thirty or forty miles per hour, you actually reduce your fuel economy by driving with open windows, because you'll increase aerodynamic drag on the car. Park in a shady spot or use a sun shade in hot weather, so you don't have to blast the air conditioning when you first get in.

14 **Don't worry about running your car's heater while driving.** Unlike other devices, the heater doesn't reduce a car's gas mileage much. The heat is generated by the engine as a byproduct of combustion, so the only electricity you're using is what's needed to run the blower motor.

15 **Don't idle your car if you can help it.** Idling consumes up to one gallon of gas per hour. After about a minute, idling will consume more gasoline than restarting the car.

16 **Start looking for a gas station when your tank is half full.** This gives you the ability to comparison shop and stop at a station with the best prices.

17 **Know your rates if you use gasoline credit cards.** Some companies offer incentives such as discounts to get you to use their cards. You might be able to save up to ten cents per gallon with such a program, but it will only be a plus if you pay off the balance each month in full. If you don't, any savings will be more than wiped out by interest charges.

18 **Don't top off your tank.** Modern cars have an antipollution evaporative emission system that includes a canister containing charcoal. This absorbs gasoline fumes from the fuel tank. When the fuel runs low, the system sucks the fumes out of the canister and injects them into the fuel mix. If the tank is overfilled, liquid gasoline can pour into the canister and destroy the charcoal, which can lead to an expensive repair of the system.

19 **Adjust your following distance for day and night.** Don't drive like your eyesight is always the same—you'll need more following distance at night between cars. In daylight, three seconds is considered a safe following distance, but at night you should increase it to five or more, especially if you're tired.

20 **When blinded by oncoming headlights, follow these precautions.** Keep your gaze down and to the right. Stay within your lane using the edge of the road or the line markings to steer by, until the headlights have passed and you can look up again. Drive at the same speed—the drivers behind you may also be temporarily blinded, and they may not see when you've stepped on your brakes. After you look back to the road, remember that it takes about six seconds for your eyes to readjust completely. And if you wear glasses, choose the kind with an antireflective coating—it cuts down on lens glare.

21 **Keep your car's interior gauge lights slightly dim.** The glow from a bright dashboard can interfere with your ability to see outside at night. If you have a choice between straining to see the gauges and straining to see the road, strain to see the gauges.

22 Don't drive at night with a dirty windshield. Grime that's a small annoyance during the day can be deadly at night, because it can cause a huge glare. Be sure you regularly clean the inside as well as the outside of your windshield.

23 Don't wait too long to turn on your headlights. Many drivers make the mistake of not turning on headlights until it's quite dark outside. Turn them on earlier than you think you need to. Even though they don't help you to see at dusk, they help other drivers to see you.

24 Keep your headlights properly adjusted. Take a moment after your headlights have been aligned to make a note of their angle. After parking your car in the garage or in front of a wall of your house, use tape to mark the ground where your car is standing, and mark the wall at the place where the brightest part of each beam hits it. Then when you park in that spot again over time, you can check and see if your lights are pointed in the same spot.

25 **Don't forget to clean the wiper blades on your windshield.** Otherwise, they'll just wipe dirt all over your windshield after you've cleaned it.

26 **Use old onion bags to clean bugs off your windshield.** The mesh should give you enough of an edge to scrape the gunk off, but it won't damage the glass. Apply a mixture of dishwashing liquid and warm water to the windshield to soften everything up, scrub with the bags, and then wipe the windshield dry with clean rags.

27 **When buying a used car seat, don't choose the oldest model.** Never buy a car seat that's more than six years old, and always make sure it isn't subject to any recalls. You can check its model number on the web page of the NHTSA: www.nhtsa.gov.

28 **When installing a car seat, read both sets of instructions first.** Make sure you look at both the manual from the manufacturer of the car seat and the owner's manual of your car. While most parents know enough to read the first, they don't realize that there may be pertinent information in the second manual as well.

29 **Aim for a snug fit when installing car seats.** A child's car seat should move no more than one inch in any direction. There are two systems for attaching a car seat: the seatbelt method and the LATCH (Lower Anchors and Tethers for Children) method. Either system is safe if followed correctly—but if you do use a LATCH system, don't use a seatbelt installation as well. Once the seat is installed, make sure your child is strapped in tightly. Harness straps should not have any slack; if you can pinch their fabric, they're too loose.

30 **Don't assume you're a pro with car-seat installation.** In a recent study by the NHTSA, new parents asked to install an infant seat did the job wrong between 95 and 100 percent of the time. More experienced users fared a bit better—but even they put the seats in too loosely about half of the time. Even more alarmingly, most of them believed they had done it correctly.

31 **Don't waste time looking for the best parking space.** People who spend time looking for an ideal parking spot, rather than just sliding into the first spot they see, spend much more time getting to the store. Not only does searching burn up time behind the wheel, but on average, it leaves you no closer to the door than anyone else.

32 **Avoid parking in the row directly across from the storefront.** People tend to park in a Christmas tree–shaped formation, with a long row straight across from the door and each row to the side becoming shorter and shorter. People who park in the row right across from the door often end up farther away from the door than those who go for the open spots off to the side.

33 **If parking is hard to find, roll down your windows.** That way, you'll hear sounds that might indicate someone is leaving: the jingling of keys, for example, or the beep of an alarm being deactivated. Be on the lookout for people with shopping bags who might be about to return to their cars.

34 **Exercise special caution driving near trucks.** Though truck drivers are equipped with large mirrors, they can only see so much. Don't drive beside a big rig if you can avoid it. If you want to know if a truck driver can see you, look for his face in the mirror. If you can't see him, then he can't see you either.

35 **Stay out of a truck's blind spot.** All trucks have a blind spot directly behind the trailer. Some drivers try to slip into this space behind a truck to save gas by riding in the truck's wake. Don't be one of them. It's dangerous, and truckers hate it. Be considerate, and don't drive where you can't be seen.

36 **If a trucker signals to change lanes, move out of the way!** Trucks can't make fast corrections, so seasoned truckers always keep an escape route open in case they need to get off the road quickly—such as if the truck's air pressure fails and the brakes suddenly lock up. Consequently, a trucker in the left lane is always looking for a way to get back to the right, where it is easier to get off the road. You can maneuver around more easily than they can, so if you see that they're looking to get into a lane, help them do it.

37 **Never drive or park on runaway truck ramps.** When driving in a mountainous area, you may have noticed the runaway truck ramps. These exist because from time to time, a truck going down a steep grade will lose its brakes and need the steep gravel ramp to stop it. On a steep grade, the momentum on a heavy loaded truck can be very high. You don't want to be in front of a truck at such a time, or pulled over in its emergency-out lane.

38 **If a truck is passing you, keep both hands on the wheel.** Passing trucks create wind gusts that can move your car to one side or another. If it's raining, be ready for a big splash too—trucks can throw up a wall of water that temporarily reduces

your visibility to zero. In short: give trucks extra space when it's windy or wet.

39 **Don't assume you can drive safely on bad roads braved by trucks.** Just as there are things you can easily do in your little car that truckers cannot—swerve in and out of traffic, parallel park, and so on—there are things a truck can do that you cannot. Because of their weight, for instance, trucks can drive on ice and snow long after your Camry has lost traction.

40 **Avoid motion sickness by looking at a nonmoving target.** In other words, look out the window at something far away. You can look at the sky, for example, about 45 degrees above the horizon. If you're in a boat, go up on deck so your eyes will experience the same cues as your ears. Avoid reading in a vehicle, and don't travel on an empty stomach—these increase your risk of queasiness.

41 **Before jump-starting a car, make sure both batteries are safe.** Look at the two car batteries you plan to link up. If the casing is damaged on either of them, if either battery is visibly leaking, or if it looks as though there is any chance the battery's solution could be frozen, don't perform the jump yourself. Call a pro.

42 **Don't be put off by a little corrosion on a car battery.** It's normal for car batteries to have a little corrosion. It should look like blue or green snow surrounding the battery terminals. Don't touch it with your bare hands—you won't blow anything up, but the chemicals can burn your skin.

43 **Know how to perform a jump start safely.** Before doing a jump start, make sure that the voltage on both batteries matches. (Unless you're getting a jump start from an old collector's car, this will probably not be an issue.) Turn off the car giving the jump, including headlights, radios, and any electrical equipment in the car. Attach one end of the red jumper cable to the dead battery's positive terminal. Then attach the other end of the cable to the positive terminal on the starting car's battery. Now attach one end of the black cable to the negative terminal of the battery of the starting car. The other end of the black cable should go onto a metal bolt on the engine block of the car with the dead battery, *not* on the battery itself.

Start the car that will be giving the jump. After about five minutes, try starting the car with the dead battery. If it doesn't start right up, turn it off and wait another five minutes before you try again.

44 **When you're jump-starting a car, don't worry if you see a few small sparks.** For this reason, you should never perform a jump start right next to a gas pump or anything that gives off fumes that could be ignited. Don't lean over the engine and gaze at the battery during this process, either. A few sparks coming out of a battery during a jump start are nothing to worry about—but if anything does go awry, you want your face to be as far from it as possible.

AROUND THE KITCHEN

1 **Read through a recipe well in advance of your meal.** Note any ingredients you will need, their amounts, and what must be done with them. Most printed recipes begin with a list of ingredients and quantities, and perhaps a cooking time. It is easy to make the mistake of reading those two pieces of information and thinking you're ready to go. But sometimes a cookbook author will sneak a crucial bit of information into the process part of the recipe—cherries that must be frozen ahead of time, for example, or meat that must be marinated for several hours.

2 **Get your ingredients together before cooking.** *Mise en place*, the French way of saying "putting in place," is a term invented by restaurant chefs for exactly this process. It ensures that there are no last-minute surprises or forgotten ingredients. Once you've gone through your recipe and noted that the carrots should be chopped, the garlic mashed, and the cheese grated, you can begin by preparing these items. Measure out the quantities you'll need, and set each aside in individual bowls or measuring cups. Doing all the prep work up front allows the cooking portion of your evening to be, well, a piece of cake!

3 **Toss leftovers after four days.** Most cooked foods last only four days when stored in an airtight container in the refrigerator. Spread the food evenly in the container so the cold air hits it consistently, and leave space between items in your refrigerator so that the cold air can circulate around them. Be aware that a food may not be safe to eat even if it has not yet started to smell bad.

4 **Keep carbonated drinks fizzy by buying them in glass bottles.** Plastic bottles are made of something called polyethylene terephthalate

(PET for short). This material is slightly permeable to the carbon dioxide gas responsible for your drink's yummy fizziness. Over time the CO_2 will escape, and if you wait long enough, your pop will be flat before you've even had a chance to open it.

5 **Don't squeeze a two-liter bottle of soda after it's opened.** It won't preserve the fizz. In fact, just the opposite will happen; the flexible container will try to return to its original shape, reducing the pressure inside the squeezed bottle. This speeds up the release of the carbonation from the liquid. Don't bother with products that promise to pump the fizz back into your soda, either. The way they work is, you screw one into your half-empty soda bottle, pump it like a tiny bicycle pump, and then seal it. Next time you open it, you hear a gratifying whoosh sound—but it's not carbonation. It's just air.

6 **Store your soda in a cool place—but not too cold.** Freezing reduces carbonation, because as the bottle freezes, the drink expands and stretches the bottle slightly out of shape. When it melts, it leaves more space in the bottle, which allows the carbon dioxide to escape from the liquid.

7 Store plastic wrap in the refrigerator or freezer. When plastic wrap is cold, it's easier to handle and less likely to stick to itself. It will quickly warm up and start clinging when you drape it over your delicious cookies.

8 To fend off freezer burn, use wrapping materials designed for freezing. The ideal packages are vacuum-sealed, thick plastic packages. If you don't have something like this, opt for freezer paper or well-fastened plastic wrap. Polyethylene wraps and sandwich bags don't do a very good job; polyethylene freezer bags are thicker and should fare better if you don't keep them too long.

9 Wrap foods properly for the freezer. Wrap foods as tightly as you can, and push all the air out of bags or wrapping. Also, do what you do when you dress for freezing temperatures: use a few layers. Uncooked red meats should be used within three months of freezing, while poultry can last as long as nine months in the freezer.

10 Feel for "snow" in frozen-food packages at the grocery store. These are ice crystals in the packaging from water that has evaporated out of the food, which means the food itself is probably now pretty dehydrated. It's still safe to eat, but it won't taste as good.

11 **If you run out of eggs, don't fret.** You can substitute a number of things for an egg: for instance, two tablespoons of milk mixed with half a teaspoon of baking powder.

12 **Ditto for sour cream and milk.** Substitute a cup of plain whole yogurt plus three tablespoons of melted butter for one cup of sour cream. In baked recipes, you can replace a cup of milk with a cup of water plus one and a half teaspoons of melted butter. (This is best for baking, though—for a lot of other uses, it's better to run out to the store for that milk.)

13 **Substitute olive oil for vegetable oil.** If you're cooking at high heat, use light olive oil, which has a similarly high smoke point to vegetable oil.

14 **Make your own sweetener substitutes.**
Brown sugar is plain sugar with molasses, and
making your own is easy. Measure one cup of
sugar for every tablespoon of molasses, and blend
well in a food processor until it looks like, well,
brown sugar. For dark brown sugar, you guessed
it—add more molasses. If you run out of honey in a
recipe, you can get by with corn syrup.

15 **Keep your brown sugar from hardening.**
Don't let the moisture out. Store it in a vapor-tight
container, like a plastic food-storage box with a
tight lid or a jar with a screw-top lid.

16 **To fix rock-hard brown sugar, restore some
of the moisture.** Seal the sugar in an airtight
container with something that gives off moisture,
like a damp towel, a piece of fruit, or a cup of
water. It will take a day or more for the sugar to be
restored to its pre-brick state. If you're in a hurry,
you can cover the sugar with a wet paper towel and
microwave it on high for a minute or two, checking
every half-minute or so to see if it's soft yet.
However, once you've heated it up, you have to use
it fast, because this is just a quick fix—the sugar will
turn into a brick again as soon as it cools.

17 **Pick the right size pan for your cake.** If your pan is too small, the cake will expand over the top and cause a mess, or bulge up in the center like a chocolate camel.

18 **For a clean finish, prepare your cake pan.** It doesn't matter how beautiful a cake is if you cannot even get it out of the pan—and if you fail to properly prepare the pan, you'll have to bail the cake out with a spoon. Most cake recipes say to grease and flour the pan before pouring in the batter. *Don't skip this step!* If you're making an especially gooey cake, line the pan with parchment paper too.

19 **When mixing cake batter, don't skip the flour sifting.** It may seem as though it's a waste of time, but sifting gets the lumps out of the flour and distributes the leavener evenly throughout the mixture, preventing dry lumps and uneven rising in your batter.

20 **Don't under- or overmix your cake batter.** If you don't take the time to thoroughly combine the flour with the other ingredients, you'll end up with swirls of ingredients in the finished cake.

On the other hand, you don't want to overmix the batter either, because if you get too much air in there, you run the risk of making the cake fall. A good rule of thumb is to fold the dry ingredients into the sugar and butter as gently as possible, then stop mixing when all of the flour has been absorbed.

21 Pop hidden bubbles in cake batter.

Smoothing the batter after pouring it into the pan works out the large air bubbles and ensures that the top of the cake bakes evenly. Here's an often-missed trick: Tap the pan with your finger or a wooden spoon to oust any remaining air bubbles trapped in the batter. If they're left in, they could cause the cake to fall or form little craters in the surface.

22 **When baking your cake, leave it alone.** Fight the urge to keep opening the oven to see how the cake is doing. When you do this, you cause the heat to fluctuate, which can cause the cake to collapse. (This is especially important with cheesecake and flourless cake.)

23 **When the cake comes out of the oven, exercise patience.** The cake needs to finish baking from within and acclimate itself to room temperature. Let it cool in the pan until the top feels firm, then turn it out onto a cooling rack. Don't frost it until it's completely cool, or your frosting will become a drippy mess. And don't rush the cooling, either—throwing the cake in the fridge to cool it quickly will only make it fall!

24 **Learn to recognize a great watermelon.** How do you tell if a watermelon has spent enough time on the vine? The larger it is, the more time it probably spent on the vine. Look at the discolored side of the outer skin. This is the side that was sitting on the soil. If it's light green, the watermelon isn't ripe and you won't get that great, juicy summer flavor. Look for a creamy yellow color there.

25 **Avoid overripe watermelons.** Watermelons are 90 percent water (hence the name), and when they are overripe their fibers start to break down. Rock the melon a little: If you hear a sloshing sound, it's overripe. If you don't hear it, rap on the rind. A ripe melon should make a hollow sound.

26 **Wash a watermelon in running water before cutting it.** Unlike most fruits, melons aren't acidic, so any bacteria you transfer from the outer surface to the inside will thrive. Be sure to refrigerate your melon within two to four hours of cutting it, too.

27 **Keep avocado-based dishes in an airtight container.** It only takes about six hours for an avocado exposed to the air to start changing color.

28 **Slow the browning of an avocado with the acid from a lemon or lime.** Besides the taste, this is why lemon juice is often an ingredient in guacamole. Dripping a bit of lemon juice on that uneaten avocado half before you wrap it up and store it could give it another day or two of green life.

29 **To stop a cut avocado from browning, immerse it in water.** Chefs who need to prepare avocados in advance of restaurant service cut them and then immediately immerse them in ice-cold water, which keeps them away from oxygen. Avocados will stay fresh this way for up to four hours in the fridge, so you can get the rest of your guac all set up and just mash in the pre-peeled and diced avocado at the last minute.

30 **Learn proper knife technique.** If you want to know the right way to use a cooking knife, watch one of the many cooking shows out there. Notice how the pros curve their fingers so they don't get cut? Use their technique as an example and keep the fingers of the hand holding the item curled back. You can even rub the flat side of the knife against your knuckles as you chop to get better control over the knife. For even greater control, use the "pinch grip." Hold the handle of the knife in your hand and tuck your middle finger against the finger-guard. With your thumb on one side and the index finger curled up on the other, pinch the heel of the blade.

31 **Chop onions in a well-ventilated room.** This will minimize the eye-watering. If that's not an option, work near the stove with the ventilation fan on. You can also chill the onion in the refrigerator before chopping it, heat the onion in the microwave for one minute before chopping it . . . or wear goggles.

32 **Keep onions longer by storing them in panty hose.** Put one onion in the leg of an old pair of panty hose and tie a knot above it. Slide another onion into the leg and tie a knot above it, and repeat. The knots keep the onions separated, which lets air circulate between them so they won't rot. When you need an onion, just cut the lowest-hanging one free.

33 **Slice a bagel horizontally.** The proper bagel-cutting technique starts with placing the bagel flat on the counter with one hand on top. Make sure your bagel is going to stay still by placing a towel or slip mat under it. Cut parallel to the counter, making sure not to curl your fingers around the bagel as you do. (For those who prefer technological solutions to problems like these, there are also special kitchen devices available for slicing bagels without resting them in the palm of your hand.)

34 **For perfect burgers, pardon a small amount of fat in the meat.** If your burgers come out dry, it may be that they started out that way. Yes, lean ground beef is good for your health, but for flavor, choose a ground chuck with about 20 percent fat. You can also accidentally dry out your meat if you knead and pack it too much. Don't try for a perfectly flat little fast food–style patty. Instead, take seven ounces of beef per patty and slap it down onto a flat, cold surface, such as a plate. Form it gently and season each side with a little salt and pepper.

35 **Grill a flavorful burger by keeping a light touch.** For perfect burger-cooking conditions, preheat your pan over a medium flame for three to four minutes and add a little oil to keep the meat from sticking. Slide the patties onto the pan and then do nothing with them for three to four minutes. (If you keep moving them around and fiddling with them, you won't get that nice even outer crust.) Before you flip the burger, check the pan. If it looks dry, add a little more oil. Approximate cooking times on the second side are two minutes for rare, three for medium-rare, four to five for medium, and six to seven for well done.

36 **For cheeseburgers, put a metal cover over the burger until the cheese is melted.** This will help you avoid that half-melted look. Just be sure not to seal the pan completely, or you'll end up with a steamed burger—which will taste a bit like something at a stadium concession stand. (Unless you're into that!)

37 **Don't reheat everything in the microwave.** Microwaves don't always do the best job of keeping yesterday's foods appetizing. You'll usually get better results reheating your leftovers in a traditional oven.

38 **Use a broiler to restore the crunch to fried foods.** Fried foods are notorious for becoming soggy in the microwave—instead, wrap your fried chicken and french fries in aluminum foil and stick them under the broiler, which provides top-down heat, and can make fried foods crunchy again.

39 **Keep your pizza crust crisp.** Leftover pizza becomes soft and doughy in the microwave, so to keep the crust crisp, bake the slices on an aluminum foil–covered baking sheet in an oven set to 450°F (232°C). Or try heating it on the stovetop. Heat a pan or skillet on medium-high for one minute; place the pizza in the pan; cover and heat for another two to three minutes. (A toaster oven also works well, if you have one.)

40 **Steam your dry leftovers.** Some leftovers, like rice or turkey, come out of the microwave tasteless and dry. To combat this problem, just add moisture. You can do this by placing a small mug filled with water, or even a damp paper towel, in the microwave with your food. This will release steam and rehydrate the leftovers. For even better flavor, skip the microwave altogether: wrap your poultry in aluminum foil and heat it in a conventional oven.

41 **Microwave leftover chips.** Leftover chips generally become inedible because they soak up too much moisture. Pop them in the microwave for thirty seconds to dry them out and give them a little more life.

42 **Don't use a microwave to make tea.** Even when microwave-heated water *looks* as though it's boiling, it's not as hot as water heated in a kettle—and boiling-hot water is needed to get all of the color and flavor of a good cup of tea.

43 **Don't take out a tea bag too soon.** The tea bag should be left in the hot water for at least two minutes, but no more than seventeen. If you drink your tea with milk, you should take out the bag after two minutes, pour the milk in, and let it sit for another six minutes before your first sip so the whole mixture can reach an ideal temperature.

FINE DINING

1 **Refine your napkin etiquette.** Once everyone at your table is seated, unfold your napkin and lay it across your lap. If you're in a really swanky place, the waiter may do this for you. When you leave the table, gather up the napkin and set it to the left of your plate. Do not leave it on the seat of your chair.

2 **Don't tear into the bread roll with your teeth.** It is considered a faux pas to bite into a whole roll or slice of bread. Rather, you should place the roll on your bread plate and then tear off bite-size pieces to butter and eat.

3 **Be prepared for a few French dining customs.** In France, diners often set their bread directly on the table in the spot where the plate would be. (Waiters on the continent use crumb collectors to sweep crumbs off the table after the bread course.) Another thing the French do differently is serve the salad after, rather than before, the main dish. The French word "entrée," which North Americans use to describe the main dish, means "entrance," and in French-speaking countries (and ritzy French restaurants everywhere), it refers to the opening course, what we might call an hors d'oeuvre.

4 **Keep from committing a cutlery gaffe.** One simple rule will save you: Start from the outside and work your way in. The fork or spoon that is farthest away from your plate should be the first used. There may be the odd exception—for example, a soup spoon may be needed before you get to the next fork on the far left—but it should be fairly obvious that even the rich don't use forks for soup.

5 **Hold your dinner fork properly.** There are two ways to hold a dinner fork. Americans generally hold the utensil in the dominant hand, with the tines pointed up. The European method keeps the fork in the left hand with the tines pointed down. Many well-traveled North Americans use the European method to demonstrate their culture and breeding—but it's not required.

6 **Only move one of your chopsticks.** The main mistake chopstick amateurs make is trying to move both of the sticks like a pair of tongs. The trick is to pinch down with only the top chopstick, using the bottom one as a base.

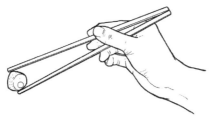

7 **Don't commit a chopsticks faux pas.** Never store your chopsticks vertically in your rice bowl when you're not using them, as this is only done at funerals. For the same reason, do not pass food to another person using chopsticks. Put the food on the other person's plate. And never ask for chopsticks in a Thai restaurant, as chopsticks are not used as utensils in Thailand.

8 **When serving, flip the chopsticks.** Use the wide end of chopsticks to take food from a communal dish. You do this for the same reason you avoid double-dipping a chip.

9 **Can't open it? Can-open it.** To open stubborn clamshell packaging, start with a can opener. Open one side of the packaging as if it were a can. The opener will not go around corners, so you can either repeat the process on each side or carefully use a utility knife—inserted into the open side, facing toward the center of the packaging—to cut the rest open.

10 **Pick up a live lobster without getting pinched.** First off, lobsters are cold-blooded, so

if you keep a lobster in icy-cold water, it's going to be a much more sluggish adversary. Come in behind the animal and seize it in one motion from above by the shell, just where the lobster's last two legs join his tail.

11 **Remove the meat from a lobster without frustration.** First, remove the legs. Grab the lobster by the back and then twist off each leg and put them aside. Now use the same twisting motion to remove the claws at the first joint. You'll need a nutcracker to get into the claw—place it around the top of the large section of the claw and squeeze firmly. Once it's open, push the meat from the top of the claw out of the end that was attached to the arm. Next, take the tail in one hand and the back in the other, and twist until the two parts separate. Once it's free, turn the tail over. Put your finger into the end of the tail that was not attached to the body. You should be able to push all of the meat out in one piece. Peel off the top and look for a long black vein—this is the digestive tract. Remove it before you eat the tail meat.

12 **Use a knife and a mallet to open crab claws,** if you don't have a nutcracker. Start by putting the claw on the table with the inside of the pincers facing up. Now place the knife slightly behind where the pincers meet. Use the mallet to tap lightly on the knife until you have cut the claw about halfway through. Do not cut it completely in half. Once you've made your cut, pick up the claw in both hands and snap it in half. This should let you pull out the claw meat with little mess. Repeat this technique on the claw arm, dip the meat in melted butter, and enjoy.

13 **Know your drinking glasses in a restaurant table setting.** Your glasses will be the ones on the right side of your plate. You may initially encounter a stunning array of up to five glasses. Your water glass will be found at the one o'clock position, right above the dinner knife. You may also have a small aperitif glass, a red wineglass, a white wineglass, and a champagne flute. Don't worry. Your server will fill the glasses that match your drink orders and remove any that are not needed.

14 **When in doubt at a restaurant, ask.** If you're at a nice restaurant, you don't really need to have much knowledge at all. Just ask your wine steward or waiter what wine he or she would recommend with the dish you've ordered. And don't be ashamed to ask the price—being shy can cost you upward of $50 a glass.

15 **Know your wine descriptors.** If a wine is said to be "brawny" or "muscular," it's a red wine with a lot of tannins and perhaps a high alcohol content. "Brooding" wines are usually red with dark fruit flavors. Their "elegant" cousins are light on the palate. You may also hear wines described as "racy," "linear," "focused," "feminine," or "austere."

16 **Pair the right wine with your food.** When it comes to food pairing, you've probably heard the rule: "Reds for red meat, whites for chicken and seafood." That's a start, but it's not always true—and there's a lot more to it. To appear savvier, make choices that won't overpower your food with the wine or lose the subtlety of a delicate wine with an overly aggressive dish. For heavy, meaty dishes with strong, spicy flavors, choose a bold red wine, like a Cabernet Sauvignon or a Malbec. If it is exceptionally rich and savory, like cheese or foie gras, try a sweet wine instead, like a Madeira. A good medium-bodied wine, such as a Pinot Noir or Merlot, pairs well with a lighter red-meat dish or stew. For lighter dishes like chicken, fish, or vegetables, try a Pinot Grigio, a dry Riesling, or a Sauvignon Blanc.

17 **Leave the cork alone when it's presented to you.** The cork presentation at a restaurant is vestigial, like your appendix. You aren't supposed to do anything about it. You can, however, glance at the cork to see if it's wet (or colored, if it's a red) partway up. This will let you know that the bottle was properly stored on its side, with the cork being constantly wet for a tight seal.

18 **Know the difference between spoiled wine and wine you just don't like.** Once the cork moment has passed, the waiter will pour a little

wine in your glass for you to sample and make sure the wine is in good condition. It may taste bad to you, but that doesn't mean it's spoiled. If you made a choice you don't particularly like, you're stuck. If a wine is spoiled, though, it will smell like vinegar or mold. Send it back.

19 **Always hold a wine glass by the stem when sampling.** This avoids warming the wine and keeps ugly fingerprints off the glass. Make small concentric circles with your glass to gently swoosh the wine around. This releases the wine's bouquet, which you can give a little sniff if you'd like.

20 **Pace yourself while indulging.** You've probably heard that mixing different types of alcoholic beverages makes you sicker than sticking with one. There's a small amount of science behind this; however, the most important factor in whether or not you get a hangover is the total amount of alcohol you consume and how fast, not what mixtures you drink.

21 **Make your martini stirred, not shaken.** Shaking a martini adds water and makes the drink weak. Martini connoisseurs will also tell you that a real martini is made with gin, not vodka. So begin with a bottle of gin, a bottle of dry vermouth, a pint glass, and lots of ice.

22 **Make sure you chill your martini sufficiently.** A memorable martini must be sufficiently chilled. Begin by filling the pint glass with ice. Next, pour in two and a half ounces of gin, followed by one half ounce of dry vermouth. Now stir. Stirring dilutes the ice just enough to chill the mix, but not enough to water it down. Another option is to pour the vermouth straight into the martini glass, swirl it, then dump it right out into the sink—this will leave a delicate whisper of the flavor behind without over-diluting the flavor of the gin.

23 **Use a chilled glass for a martini.** When you've gone to all the trouble of making a martini the right way, the last thing you want to do is ruin it by pouring it into a warm glass. If your glass is room temperature, the liquid's temperature will rise, and you'll lose the whole chilly effect. Plan ahead by putting the glasses in the freezer, or chill them by filling them with ice just before you start to mix your drinks. Also, choose the right glassware: A vintage-size (four-to-six-ounce) glass is perfect. Larger glasses just let the cocktail warm up before you finish drinking it.

24 **Garnish your martini properly, with a twist of lemon.** Start by cutting the ends off your lemon. To separate the fruit from the rind, slip a spoon between the rind and the fruit and run it around the lemon on both ends. Lay the hollowed out rind on its side and make one long cut so you can flatten it out. Now roll it up tightly. Push a toothpick through the rind to hold the roll in place. Now you can slice through the rind to create twists. An average lemon will yield about eight twists. Before you artistically place the twist, rub the peel gently over the rim of the glass so your guest will taste the oils when sipping the cocktail.

SHOPPING AND BARGAIN HUNTING

1 **Get to know the clerks at your favorite clothing stores.** Clerks are always happy to do a good job for a repeat customer. Once they get to know your taste, they'll keep an eye out for the kind of clothing you like and let you know about upcoming sales.

2 **Build your wardrobe on a solid base.** Invest in at least one high-quality piece of clothing that is not simply trendy and will last for years. Use this as a base and pair it with inexpensive, washable clothing that you get from the clearance rack or secondhand store.

3 **Never pay the first price on a piece of clothing.** Early in each season, a department store will put a dress out on display with a preprinted price tag. Only 10 to 20 percent of buyers actually pay this price. (Thank them—they subsidize the rest of us!) As the season wears on, the dress will be marked down further and further, until it ends up on the clearance rack. Try to make sure one of these lower prices is the one you end up paying for it.

4 **Shop for clothes on Thursdays.** Shopping experts suggest hitting stores on Thursdays to get items before they're depleted during weekend sales. (You can usually go back once the sale begins and get discounts applied retroactively.)

5 **Look for discount versions of your favorite items.** One of the great secrets of the fashion industry is that clothing manufacturers often create two versions of their trendy new duds: one for regular stores and the other for discount shops. A blouse may be exactly the same, but shipped with two different labels, for these two destinations. You can find these duplicates by looking for a code that identifies the garment's manufacturer. On the tag of every piece of clothing you will find the letters "RN" followed by several numbers. Write down the RN number of the garment you like at the department store, then look for the same RN number at the discount store. If the numbers are the same, so is the manufacturer.

6 **Always ask for discounts.** You may be able to get a discount you weren't aware of, just by asking. It doesn't always work, but when you're checking out, always ask, "Are there any discounts available on this item?" Worst-case scenario, there aren't, and the clerk looks at you a little funny. Best-case scenario, you'll save some money.

7 **Swap convenience foods for a few low-cost recipes.** It'll save you money to spring for raw ingredients rather than pre-packaged meals. Also, be open to variety—that way, if you plan for pork and discover that your local shop is having an incredible sale on beef, you can take the bargain and prepare a meal with what's on sale.

8 **Keep track of product pricing at different stores in your area.** You might keep a price book with sections that correspond to the aisles in a typical grocery store, or try to arrange the items alphabetically—apples followed by apricots, and so on. Use whatever system makes sense to you. You'll soon become familiar enough with the prices to know if a product has been marked up or down.

9 **Visit different stores for different things.** Chances are, no one store in your area has the best prices on everything—and after a while, you'll start to see the patterns. (These days you can also find smartphone applications that allow you to find out where the best deals are on individual products.)

10 **Plan meals before making your grocery list.** Know what you need for the meals you want to make, and set realistic upper limits on prices for the items you buy regularly. Decide which stores to go to based on which are likeliest to have the best prices for the major items on your list. If you discover that those items are priced higher than you're willing to pay, pass them up and shop for a different meal.

11 **Use coupons wisely.** Coupons are useful if they help you to save money on items you would normally buy, but not if they entice you to buy things you usually don't. Instead of just clipping coupons, stop and chat with the staff at the stores where you shop. They can give you insider information about what days new stock comes in, or when prices are changed—and they won't let you miss the most useful coupons in the circular.

12 **Shop intelligently for a used car.** Focus your search on cars that are two to four years old. By then, cars have depreciated enough in price to save you money, but still have a lot of life left in them. And in addition to dealerships and private sellers, don't forget to check out public auctions— you can often find great deals on repossessed vehicles there.

13 **Look to the best sources for car information.** Before you start car shopping, read Consumer Reports and look for pricing information in the Kelley Blue Book. You should be able to find these online or at your local library. The National Highway Traffic Safety Administration (NHTSA) also keeps records on recalls and crash-test results. For used cars, there are services such as AutoCheck and Carfax, which maintain databases with vehicle histories. Using the VIN number, these services will tell you whether a car was ever damaged in a fire or flood, repurchased under a state "lemon law," or totaled. A database search on a car can also reveal odometer fraud.

14 **Know what you need in a car, versus what you want.** You may *want* a silver car with a great stereo and a sunroof, but what you *need* is a reliable car with great gas mileage. Be sure to keep these distinctions in mind, so you don't become distracted from the important stuff by extras like power windows and cup holders.

15 **Pick a strategic time for car shopping.** Try to do your car shopping in the evening in the last

week of the month, in late fall or winter. Sales are slowest in that season, and you can usually get the best deals then. The last week of the month is when dealerships are under the most pressure to make their sales quotas, and by evening each day, many salespeople are tired and ready to go home, so they're apt to be more flexible about closing deals.

16 **Look for damage in a used car.** Try to shop for a used car on a clear day, because rain can hide a vehicle's surface imperfections. (These might indicate that the car has been in an accident.) Look inside the trunk and make sure the paint color there matches that of the body. If it doesn't, or if the doors, trunk, or hood don't open easily, there's a good chance the car was in an accident at some point.

17 **To get a good price on a car, try asking a couple of inside questions.** If you've found a car that you love but you can't quite rise to the price the salesman is quoting, try asking, "What's your holdback on that car?" You're asking what their markup is, and it shows you're in the know. You can also ask what the invoice is. The invoice is the price at which the dealership bought the car. Of course, dealers need to make a living, too, so even if they're willing to tell you this number, they probably won't offer you that price—but you'll be closer to knowing the absolute lower limit at which they can sell it.

18 **Inspect a car's coolant before you test-drive it.** While the vehicle is still completely cold, look at the cooling system by unscrewing the radiator cap and siphoning off a little fluid with an antifreeze tester. The coolant should be translucent, not murky or cloudy. If it's either of those, the radiator may be corroded.

19 **Know what to look for during a test drive.** Make sure no warning lights stay on. Check the

accelerator and brake for responsiveness. Make sure the car holds its line on the road and doesn't veer to one side or the other. Listen for telltale squeaks and noises: A persistent click under heavy acceleration could mean the lifters or rods are worn, which requires an expensive engine overhaul to fix. Pay attention to the transmission and see if the car has trouble engaging when accelerating. Be sure to drive somewhere shaded or dark so you can take a look at the headlights and be sure they're bright enough. After you've driven the car, look underneath for leaks.

20 **Before buying a car, take it to your favorite garage and have them do a pre-purchase inspection.** Your mechanic can do a compression test to evaluate the output from each cylinder of the engine, potentially saving you from having to do some very expensive repairs in the near future. Also, have the mechanic take a look at the brake disc pads and drums. These could be worn without producing sponginess or squeaking noises. The mechanic can also test the electrical system with a diagnostic machine.

HEALTH AND BEAUTY

1 **If your nail-polish technique is shaky, start with a clear coat or subtle solid color.** Most people won't pay enough attention to your fingers to notice if you've messed up a bit—unless you have smeared bright red all over your cuticles.

2 **For perfect nail polish, apply petroleum jelly to the skin around your nails.** That way, if you screw up, you can easily wipe away any paint that went off your nails. You'll be left with a nice, neat manicure. (And as an added bonus, the petroleum jelly will have softened your cuticles!)

3 **Get used to heels before you go out in them.**
If you're unaccustomed to walking in high heels,
don't wait for your big night to strap on those
four-inch heels. Shoe experts suggest you spend
at least two hours walking in them to let the fabric
stretch to accommodate the shape of your foot.
Then, before you go out, spend twenty minutes
walking in them around your house.

4 **Take tiny steps in heels, not long
strides.** And don't expect to move as
quickly as you do in your gym shoes.
Pointing your feet outward slightly
will help you keep your balance.

5 **Steer clear of too-high heels.**
The higher the heel, the more danger to your
foot health and balance, so choose lower heels
for everyday wear. Only unbox your stunning
stilettos—if you must—for a few hours at a time.

6 **Use plenty of sunscreen.** Be sure to get a nice,
even coat, and apply it again after you swim or
sweat. But don't rely on sunscreen alone to keep
you protected from the sun. Keep your shoulders

covered, and wear a hat with a big brim. You may not look like the models in a swimsuit catalog, but you'll avoid a painful sunburn and have healthier skin for life.

7 **Beware of sun exposure, even when it's not particularly sunny out.** You can get sunburned on an overcast day, or in the winter when the sun reflects off of snow and ice. The only thing you need to get sunburned is prolonged exposure to ultraviolet rays—and these aren't always visible.

8 **See the doctor about suspicious beauty marks.** Even one blistering sunburn can double your risk of developing melanoma, an often-lethal form of skin cancer. If you spot a suspicious mole, go straight to the doctor to check things out. Early detection leads to a greater survival rate.

9 **Choose dark blue or red shirts for sun protection.** When researchers dyed lightweight cotton different shades of blue, red, and yellow, then measured the amounts of UV rays that were able to penetrate them, they discovered that darker colors blocked out more than lighter shades.

10 **Invest in quality tattoos.** One of the biggest mistakes potential tattoo-ees make is to go with the cheapest artist. Tattoo removal is expensive, and you don't want to have to pay for the tattoo twice by having to get a better artist to touch it up or cover it up entirely. You'll spend less in the long run by saving up now and getting just what you want—not what you *almost* want.

11 **Find the right tattoo artist for the design you want.** When selecting something as personal and permanent as a tattoo, you would think people would put in at least as much time and thought as they do in purchasing a car. Instead, many people walk into the first tattoo studio they see and hire the first artist they talk to. But no one excels at everything. Some artists are great at tribal tattoos, but not as gifted at three-dimensional skulls. Ask around and check online to find the right person for your job.

12 **Get your tattoo in a spot that's easily concealable with clothing.** That way you don't have to worry about any social or work repercussions. Try to imagine the design in different outfits and contexts. You might love the dragon on your arm when you're at the beach, but will you be as happy with it when you're wearing a sleeveless dress at a wedding?

13 **Avoid ephemeral tattoo imagery.** You should probably not tattoo the name of your favorite band on yourself. Will One Direction rock forever? Imagine this were 1983—you might have felt the same way about Kajagoogoo. Who? Exactly.

14 **When getting a tattoo, don't forget: your body is going to change.** Try to imagine what that Celtic knot on your hip would look like if you put on a few extra pounds. Skin also changes as you age, and finely detailed tattoos can spread and become fuzzy. Ask your artist for tips on which designs are likely to last longest. If you're set on something intricate, plan on some way to touch it up later that will hide any blown-out details. Ladies: consider the changes that your body will go through if you decide to have children. (Women are more likely than men to express regret over a tattoo.) Tattoos on the abdomen can be drastically stretched and changed by a pregnancy; a cute gecko can become Godzilla. That said, you can avoid the worst ravages by applying cocoa butter to your tattoo a couple of times a day throughout the pregnancy—things will still stretch, but they won't get destroyed.

15 **When in doubt, choose dark colors for your tattoo.** Dark inks are the easiest to remove later with lasers.

16 **Know what those Asian characters say before you etch them into your skin.** Many people sport what has been called "gibberish font"—characters that supposedly say "peace" in Japanese but actually say "sushi," or worse. If your tattoo artist offers to spell out your name letter by letter using corresponding Japanese or Chinese characters, he doesn't have a clue as to what he is writing—those languages don't work that way.

17 **Apply makeup in a complementary color to conceal a black eye.** Hiding a shiner with makeup is hard, but try a yellow-green liquid or cream concealer if you're working on a fresh bruise. It may seem counterintuitive, but these shades will offset the red and blue of the shiner. Dab on the makeup and spread it evenly. After it dries, you may need a second coat. After that dries, apply a foundation that matches your skin tone.

18 **Prolong the life of your razor by soaking it in mineral oil.** The oil will slow the corrosion that dulls the cutting edge. When you're finished soaking the razor, dip the corner of a cloth in rubbing alcohol and wipe the oil off.

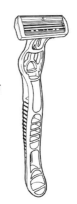

19 **Change your razorblade or toss out your disposable razors regularly.** For cheap disposable razors, "regularly" may be as often as every third shave.

20 **Don't apply shaving foam directly onto a dry face.** Doing that will give you a shredded chin. Instead, wet the skin with hot water or apply moisturizing skin cream before you lather up. You could also shave directly after taking a bath or shower.

21 **Rinse your razor regularly throughout the shave.** Those little bits of beard gum up the works, and your instinct will be to push down even harder to compensate, which can cause cuts.

22 **Try a fancier shaving cream.** Shaving cream from a can is fine, but if you want a really good shave, opt for a glycerin-based cream from a tub, which you put on with a quality shaving brush. A shaving brush exfoliates your skin and makes the whiskers stand out while providing a richer, more hydrating lather. Apply an even layer to the entire beard area. Avoid damaging the shaving brush's bristles by storing it with the bristles upright.

23 **Brush your teeth for the proper length of time.** You should brush for a full two minutes—120 seconds—in order to have healthy gums and minty-fresh breath. It doesn't sound like a long time, but most people spend less than 30 seconds brushing!

24 **Brush your teeth regularly.** In a world run by dentists, you would be brushing your teeth three times a day: when you get up in the morning, after lunch, and just before you go to bed. The middle brushing tends to get skipped because people are at work, but if you want your pearly whites to last a lifetime, keep a travel brush at work and pop into the restroom for a quick clean on your lunch break.

25 **Clean your tongue.** This will get rid of swamp breath. You can either use your toothbrush or buy a special tongue cleaner for the purpose. Nowadays a lot of toothbrushes come with special tongue-scraping ridges on the backs of their heads, so you can often get both in one.

26 **Only use mouthwash if you like the feel of it.** Otherwise, you might just as well rinse with water. According to the Food and Drug Administration (FDA), there is no proof that mouthwash gives you healthier gums or cleaner teeth than rinsing with plain water.

27 **Don't use toothbrushes with natural bristles.** They sound good, but they're actually gross, because natural fibers trap bacteria. Buy brushes with synthetic-fiber bristles—they'll be nonporous, and the bacteria will be easier to rinse away.

28 **Keep toothbrushes separate.** Allowing your toothbrush to mingle with your family's brushes can cause germs to migrate to everyone. Store brushes upright and not touching. They'll dry properly, and everyone will keep their mouth germs to themselves.

29 **Replace your toothbrush whenever you get sick.** Germs can survive on your brush and reinfect you, so don't keep your toothbrush after you've been sick—it can make you sick again. (And no matter how healthy you are, you should replace your toothbrush every three months.)

IN THE WARDROBE

1 **Don't be misled by "dry clean only" labels.**
Even if it says "dry clean only," there's a good
chance you can hand-wash the item and save time
and money in the process. Many garments made
of silk, satins, nylon, and even woolens and rayon
can be gently hand-washed. And some "dry clean
only" clothing shouldn't be dry cleaned at all. If
a garment isn't soiled, dry cleaning doesn't do a
good job of removing perspiration and oils from
an everyday office shirt.

2 **Don't wring out wet "dry clean only"
clothes that you've hand-washed.** Rayon is
especially prone to coming out a bit stiff and fuzzy
if it's agitated too much. Once you've rinsed the

clothes, don't throw them in the dryer. Lay them flat on a drying screen instead. If you really miss that freshly pressed look, you can still hand-wash your delicate clothes and then take them to the cleaners for a professional press from time to time.

3 **Don't dry clean a piece of clothing every time you wear it.** Your clothes won't last any longer if you dry clean them rather than hand-washing them. Dry cleaning can also damage buttons and eventually deteriorate fabric, so you should really only take a "dry clean only" garment in for cleaning when it's soiled. Keep your clothes wrinkle-free and aired out by hanging them up as soon as you take them off.

4 **Don't use too much laundry detergent.** Most people guess how much laundry detergent they need, or just fill the cap up to the top. That wastes more than half of the loads a detergent bottle could wash. Extra suds in the machine can also lead to the development of odor-causing residue, and can cause high-efficiency machines to use extra water and extend the cycle length, which costs you even more money.

5 **Remove stains without making them worse.** Don't work from the center, where the stain is deepest, to the outside. This can cause the stain to spread. Instead, start from the outer edges and work your way in. If you don't have a spot remover handy, try a solution of two parts water to one part rubbing alcohol. (Simply soaking your stained clothes overnight in warm water should help get the stains out, too.)

6 **Sort your clothes according to their ideal washing cycle.** Check the washing instructions on clothing labels, and change the settings on your washing machine accordingly. As a general rule, clothes that are soiled with body oils are best washed with hot water; colored clothes should be washed in cold water to keep them from running and losing pigment.

7 **Brighten whites in cold water.** If you want to really brighten your whites, add a spoonful of cream of tartar to the cold wash water. And you already know not to wash that bright-red skirt in the same load as your white shorts, right? If you do have an item that's likely to bleed, soak it in salt water before washing it, or add a dash of vinegar to the wash cycle, to keep its color from spreading to lighter garments.

8 **Wash wool sweaters by hand.** Always keep this fact in mind: It's not heat but agitation that causes shrinkage. This means that even when you wash by hand, you need to avoid too much rubbing, kneading, and swishing. Washing a sweater, therefore, does not require a lot of work. A more apt description might be soaking.

9 **Take your time hand-washing a sweater.** Pour about a quarter-cup of detergent into your sink and fill it with hot or warm water. Shampoo and liquid dish soap also work. Submerge your garment in the soapy water until it's soaked all the way through, then *do nothing*. Leave the sweater in the water for about half an hour. When you come back, remove the sweater from the water and gently press out the excess water. Then refill the sink with cold water. Put the sweater back in the water and let it soak for another half-hour. Repeat this step one more time to rinse out all of the remaining soap.

10 **Never put a wet sweater in the dryer.** The heat won't harm it, but the tumbling might. Don't be tempted to twist or wring out the sweater, either. When you're done soaking it, take the sweater out of the water and lay it out flat on a large towel. Cover it with another towel, and roll all three up together. Press on the roll to push out more of the water. Finally, unroll the sweater and put it on a drying rack. (If you don't have one, set it on another towel to dry.) After a few hours, come back and flip the sweater to let the back side dry. If you like, when the sweater has fully dried you can tumble it in the dryer briefly to soften it up.

11 **Try to unshrink a tiny sweater.** Immerse the shrunk sweater in a solution of water and hair conditioner for half an hour. With any luck, the fibers will untangle and your sweater will magically expand to its original size.

12 **Don't wait to fix a snagged sweater.** Repairing a sweater snag is easy, as long as you act quickly. If you don't, the snag will unravel the knit at a surprising rate, and then you might not be able to fix it at all. First, take your sweater off and turn it inside out. Look at the snag and see if you can identify where it started. Do *not* pick up the scissors! If you cut the snagged loop, you will most likely end up with a big hole. You'll need a crochet hook to perform this repair by the book; depending on the size of the loop, you may also need some thread. (Manufacturers sometimes include some extra thread for just such an emergency.) Using your crochet hook, or a reasonable substitute, ease the snagged loop through to the inside (now outside) of the sweater. Be sure you pull it through the same hole that it came out of, or you'll create a new stitch and pucker the fabric. Turn the sweater right-side-out for a moment to check your work. If you've done everything right, the hole will be gone and the snag will be invisible. Good job! Now turn the sweater back the other way. Tie a knot in the loop from the snag. If it's large, you can snip the part above the knot away with scissors. If it's too small to knot, you'll have to thread a needle with the matching thread you found (or bought), and carefully sew the loop flat.

13 **Keep some liquid ravel preventer handy.**
This is an adhesive safe for knit fabrics, and is
the best first aid for snagged sweaters. Apply
it once you've pulled the loop in (see #12), then
turn the sweater right-side-out again and gently
stretch it to smooth out any bunching. Or, if you're
someplace where you have access to an iron, press
both sides of the garment over a cotton cloth with
the iron set to "Wool," and you're done.

14 **Improvise what you need to fix sweater
snags.** If you can't find a crochet hook, take
a paper clip, unwind it, and fashion it into a
makeshift one. If you don't travel with a supply of
thread, you may find some near the seams at the
bottom of your sweater. You only need a tiny bit.
If you don't have liquid ravel preventer, clear nail
polish can serve as a backup.

15 **Fight yellow pit stains at their source—
your deodorant.** You probably assumed that
the yellow stains under the arms of your T-shirts
were caused by your potent sweat. It turns
out that they're caused by the aluminum from
antiperspirants, combined with the salt in your
sweat. If you're able to find an effective non-

aluminum antiperspirant, your yellow-pit-stain problem should clear up. You might try a powder like Gold Bond, which can reduce wetness without using aluminum.

16 **Don't reach for the bleach to get rid of pit stains.** Chlorine bleach makes pit stains even worse. Instead, try an oxygen-based bleach such as OxiClean, or a stain remover specially formulated to remove sweat stains. A great home remedy is to mix one part baking soda to one part hydrogen peroxide to one part water. Rub the solution on the stains and let it set for at least thirty minutes before washing.

17 **If you've had a sweaty day, wash your shirt right away.** Don't let a sweaty shirt sit in the hamper. And if it shows some yellowing when it comes out of the wash, don't put it in the dryer. Instead, line-dry the shirt—in the sun, if you can.

18 **If nothing gets rid of your pit stains, use disposable underarm shields.** These stick directly to the inside of the shirt to soak up sweat, and can be thrown away after use. Or you could just switch to dark-colored shirts. They'll still get stained by the salt and aluminum mixture, but at least no one will see.

19 **Don't add fabric softener while washing your towels.** It can make them less absorbent. If you already doused them in the stuff before reading this, you can bring them back by adding a cup of distilled vinegar to the rinse cycle. (And in fact, if you like homemade solutions, you can save money by replacing fabric softener with vinegar altogether—just make sure you have a good rinse cycle so you don't go around smelling like salad dressing.)

20 **Try going soapless with your laundry.** There are those who argue that detergent is not necessary at all, and that it's actually the agitation in the washing machine that cleans clothes, just by pushing them around in the water. If you're feeling adventurous—or if you just want to try not spending money on detergent—give it a try and see if you notice a difference!

21 **Fix a nonfunctional zipper.** If you find that your zipper just won't zip, the slider is probably worn or bent out of shape. The slider is also to blame if the zip seems welded in place. The main way that a slider gets bent is by fabric getting caught in the mechanism, so don't just start yanking away. Try to gently pull the threads out of the slider or the zipper's teeth. If you still can't get it open, try greasing the zipper with candlewax, soap, or lip balm.

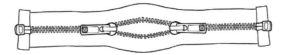

22 **Fix a zipper slider with a pair of pliers.** Gently squeeze the slider back into shape with the pliers. You want to squeeze it just enough to keep it from sliding down the teeth, or open it just enough to allow it to move freely—not enough to seal it shut or break it in half. If the zipper is missing teeth or is coming off the fabric altogether, the fix is more complicated and requires some sewing skill.

23 **Learn to interpret the hieroglyphics on ironing instructions.** These symbols are all variations on a little iron symbol. If you're not supposed to iron it at all, the little iron has an X over it. If the iron has dots in it, they correspond to the number of clicks on your iron's thermostat. If you see two dots on the icon, set the real iron to the two-dot setting.

24 **Use the right iron temperature.** Ironing things with too cool an iron is not disastrous, just ineffective. Ironing with too hot an iron can cause woolen fibers to become shiny, and may cause manmade fibers to melt.

25 **Clean out a gunked-up iron.** If you find that you have a gunky iron, lay out a piece of aluminum foil and iron it. The buildup should stick to the foil after a few passes. That gunk comes from touching a hot iron to synthetic fabric, causing the fibers to melt and coat the iron in the liquid material. Every time you fire up the iron from that point on, it will melt a bit of the gunk and transfer it to anything else it touches—until you fix it.

26 **Don't iron a dirty shirt.** Stains get set forever that way.

27 **Iron clothes while they're still a bit damp from washing.** Remove clothes you want to iron from the dryer, or take them off the line before they're completely dry. If the item is entirely dry, spray it with a light mist of water from a spray bottle before ironing.

28 **If you're skipping the iron, fold clothes right out of the dryer.** If you miss that window, you may want to run the dryer on warm for a few minutes to loosen up the clothing before folding.

JOB-HUNTING

1 **Make sure any public social media profiles have an appropriate photo.** "Your photo is your virtual handshake, so upload a photo that aligns with your role as a professional but also makes you seem approachable," says Catherine Fisher, a San Francisco-based LinkedIn career expert.

2 **Leave the right information on networking sites like LinkedIn.** List more than one prior position—profiles with multiple prior positions tend to be viewed up to 29 times more often. When writing about your past jobs, passion projects, volunteer gigs, and schooling, consider every experience in terms of the skills you gained. Add a lot of details about the region you live: More than 30 percent of recruiters conduct advanced searches based on location, so the more details you have about the region where you live, the more likely it is that you'll be found and connected with your next opportunity.

3 **Get a customized public-profile URL.** "When you created your LinkedIn profile, it probably had some ugly combination of letters, numbers, and backslashes that had no value for your personal branding," says Larry Kim, a business contributor to Inc.com. Update this to reflect your name—it'll sell you better online. The same is true of your personal or professional website. If possible, pay the extra web hosting fee to shorten the URL to only your name.

4 **Add a good long summary to your public profile.** A summary of forty words or more makes your profile more likely to turn up in a future employer's search. "A good tip is to ensure your summary includes keywords and skills featured in desirable job descriptions for your field," says Larry Kim of Inc.com.

5 **Boost your real-world work relationships online.** Sites like LinkedIn and Facebook can help you keep track of the people in your network. LinkedIn even has a Relationship section that allows you to write notes about a contact, or to set reminders to "check in" with them at various intervals. And if you don't have any recommendations yet, don't be shy about asking for them. "LinkedIn makes it super easy, providing an 'Ask to be recommended' link," Larry Kim of Inc.com says. "Pick specific people. Don't just randomly ask all your contacts."

6 **Download your social media connections.** After you've gone to all the trouble of building a large professional network, you don't want to risk losing everyone's contact info if your social media platform crashes or collapses. Nearly all social media sites offer an option to download followers, friends, or connections as a .CSV file via the Settings page. Search "export contacts" in the FAQ for your particular social media platform to locate step-by-step instructions.

7 **Don't overshare by placing your full résumé online.** This is especially important if your résumé lists your phone number. "There are too many untrustworthy people and staffing firms out there that will download your résumé, add it to their databases, and even submit to their clients without your permission," says Amanda Neiser, a Long Island–based recruiter and founder of Plum Placements, Inc.

8 **Make it easy for a recruiter to imagine you in the job.** Your résumé should have a title at the top. This doesn't have to be your current job title—think about what you would answer if someone asked you what you do for a living. If you'd say, "I'm a marketing manager," that's your title. Follow it with a brief profile that quickly sums up who you are and, most importantly, what you have to offer.

9 **Customize your résumé for each application.** Too many job searchers put all of their attention into creating one résumé and then refuse to change it. Get in the habit of customizing it for each company to which you apply. Read up on the company's mission and values, learn as much as you can about the position and what function you would serve there, and then tweak your résumé to show exactly how your particular skills and experience fit the need.

10 **Follow directions carefully when applying for jobs.** If you have a beautiful functional résumé and Company X asks you to submit a chronological résumé following its online template, then you have to do that—even if you think your résumé highlights your talents better. Don't assume that you're so wonderful that they'll make an exception and accept your emailed functional résumé instead of what they've asked for—what you're really doing is automatically disqualifying yourself from the job.

11 **Get specific in a job application.** Don't just say that you're a "self-motivated, hard-working team player with attention to detail." Tell them specifically what you mean by those terms, and let your accomplishments speak for themselves. Don't think you have any accomplishments? Think again. It's all in how you word it. Instead of saying, "I did effective cold calling for an advertising agency," say "I initiated 200 calls a day, which led directly to the acquisition of thirty new accounts, including three of the agency's largest clients."

12 **Avoid using the expression "entry-level" in your objective statement.** This is good advice even if you really are just starting out. The phrase screams, "I don't have any experience, but you can get me cheap!" It may be true, but why make it the first thing you say about yourself? Instead, maximize your experience—you probably have more work experience than you think. You don't have to focus only on paid work in the career field you're trying to enter. Did you lead a team as part of a volunteer project? Were you in ROTC? Think about everything you learned and the skills you used. There is a good chance you'll find some experience that can be applied to the job.

13 **Get some honest critique of your résumé before you send it out.** Have a friend look it over for you. You might have looked at it six times and still not noticed that you listed your current job as "Copy Editer." A fresh set of eyes can catch embarrassing misspellings and minor things you may have overlooked.

14 **Be prepared for a job interview.** Read up on your prospective employer on the web and through industry magazines. Have an idea of the company's mission and objectives so that you can express how your particular talents will be an asset. Quiz yourself on some of the most commonly asked interview questions. (You can find these online pretty easily.) Have printouts of your résumé, make sure you know how to get to the office, try on your outfit the night before, and bring some mints to suck on before you go in. Take a deep breath! You'll be fine.

15 **Rehearse your interview answers.** Long before you're asked the first question in an interview, you should have rehearsed your pitch. Write out a sixty-second "commercial" about your reasons for pursuing the position and why you'd be a good fit. Make it specific to the job. Don't memorize it word for word, but read it enough to internalize all the main points. This will be your answer when the interviewer opens with, "Tell me about yourself." Don't go on and on—you want the interviewer to discover new and wonderful things about you as the interview progresses.

16 **Dress for the job—plus a little extra.** If you're going to an office interview, you want to go for a tasteful suit instead of business casual.

17 **Give a good handshake.** It should be about three seconds and be firm but not too tight. In North America, you should shake two or three times; in some parts of Europe, a single firm shake is more customary. To cultivate warm feelings in your handshake partner, gently touch his wrist with your forefinger. Aim for the spot where you would take a pulse. Gently touching this sensitive spot tends to foster a feeling of closeness, even though the recipient is generally not aware of the reason for it.

18 **Be self-possessed at your interview.** Don't seat yourself first. Remain standing until you're greeted by the interviewer, in order to make the best first impression. (You don't want her first

impression to be of you getting your things in order and adjusting your clothing.) If you have a briefcase or portfolio with you, hold it in your left hand. This leaves your right hand free to shake without any awkward shuffling or pauses.

19 **Don't take out your nerves or frustrations on an assistant.** Remember, your interviewer works closely with this person. You don't want him to say, "That guy was kind of rude," when you're out of earshot. Thanking the assistant can go a long way.

22 **Don't be humble in your interview.** Be confident and engaging. Sit straight in the middle of your chair with one arm on the armrest and the other on the table. You'll look and feel more confident. Speak freely about your accomplishments and skills.

23 **Answer questions carefully.** If you draw a blank during an interview, ask the interviewer to rephrase the question. It's much better to ask for clarification than to ramble through an incoherent half-answer. And if you're tempted to give a yes-man answer, don't. Interviewers are smart enough to know when you're just telling them what they want to hear.

24 **Don't forget to thank your interviewer.**
Finish your meeting with a firm handshake and say something like, "I really appreciate you taking the time to talk to me about this position."

25 **Write your interviewer a thank-you note.**
Do this within a day of your interview. Your note can either be written by hand and sent through the mail, or typed and emailed. Email is faster, but your message will stand out more if you send it the old-fashioned way. (By the way, your "thank-you" message will not be nearly as effective if your prospective employer's name is spelled wrong—so be sure to take a business card on your way out of the interview.)

AT THE WORKPLACE

1 **Take regular breaks from the computer at work.** Some experts suggest the 30-30-30 rule: For every thirty minutes of computer work, gaze thirty feet away for thirty seconds. Others have proposed a 20-20-20 rule; the idea is the same. The main point is that you need to give your eyes regular breaks. Stop what you're doing for a short time and look at something in the distance.

2 **While working at a computer, don't forget to blink.** Studies show that people who work at computers blink less frequently than normal, which leads to dry eyes. Lubricating eyedrops can help—but it's better just to remember to blink!

3 **Assign a deadline to every task on your to-do list.** This helps circumvent procrastination. Tell yourself you need it done by Wednesday, and vow to stick to it. Then when your Wednesday self sees the task in front of her, she'll be much less likely to insist she'll do it on Thursday.

4 **Don't become overwhelmed by your to-do list.** People do all the time. This is because they expect it to get finished. It won't. When you check one thing off, there will be a new thing to do. Remember that the purpose of a to-do list is to get the tasks out of your short-term memory so you can be more effective—it's not to finish everything you'll ever have to do so you can retire to a life of utter leisure. That'd be asking an awful lot from a to-do list.

5 **Don't try to keep more than five to nine things in mind at once.** Our brains are unable to do it. Write down, "Go to the post office," and don't worry about it again until it's time to tackle that task. Checking off the item will feel even better than the guilty pleasure of putting it off.

6 **Be aware of the mental games you play to put off tasks.** It'll better enable you to come up with countermeasures. Remember, if you don't feel like doing something today, chances are you won't be any more inclined to do it tomorrow. If you really want to learn Spanish or read Proust, you might as well start now.

7 **Don't print every little email and memo.** People feel less wasteful and guilty printing things out when they put the paper in a blue recycling bin afterward—but they shouldn't. Remember that recycling doesn't achieve a one-to-one ratio. It

takes a lot of energy to remake paper, and each sheet of paper you recycle doesn't magically turn into a clean sheet. Conserving paper is one step better than recycling.

8 **Don't discard paper that has a blank side.** Instead, put it in a box by your desk. You can reach for this paper for note-taking, or for your everyday, utilitarian print jobs. Just don't put anything in your reuse box that you wouldn't want just anyone to read—you don't want to print out directions for your coworker, only to have her realize that it's printed on the back of a steamy sex scene from your novel-in-progress, or a spreadsheet with the salaries of everyone in the office.

9 **Use generic and refurbished printer-ink cartridges.** With a quick search online, you can usually find all manner of these cartridges, which tend to be much cheaper than manufacturer brands. But read the reviews! Although it seems thrifty to buy them, some of them can be unreliable. If you have a steady hand, you might also try an ink-refill kit to refill your old cartridges. They work, and offer great savings—if you're not afraid of the messy process.

10 **Don't print in color unless you really need to.** Color prints are great for eye-catching presentations, business cards, flyers, and photo printing. Yet most of the time, printing in color is just a waste of ink.

11 **Don't waste pages printing from the web.** Have you ever tried to print an article from the internet and been startled when it came out of the printer with ten pages of comments and brilliant-color promotions and ads? There are free web services that allow you to isolate the elements you need and print only those. Or you can highlight the text you want with your cursor, right-click, and select "Print." Alternatively, copy and paste it into a word-processor document. Any of these methods can save you a lot of ink and paper.

12 **Don't re-print pages with folded edges or staples in the corners.** If you run such paper through the printer, you may end up spending your day fixing paper jams.

13 **Keep your mood positive at work.** Mood affects your ability to focus. If you know you're going to have a big (or potentially dull) meeting

the following day, be sure to get enough sleep, and try to go into the room in a good mood.

14 **If your focus is drifting at work, put yourself in a "peak state."** Sit or stand up straight, throw your shoulders back, and lift your head. This will get oxygen pumping through your body more easily, and focus your attention.

15 **In a boring meeting, look for something of value—even if it's indirect.** If the conversation involves a completely unrelated department or work process, and you're baffled as to why you're there, pretend you're a film critic and the meeting is a movie. Make mental notes about all of the things the facilitator is doing right and wrong.

This should at least keep your focus within the room, and prevent you from drifting off.

16 **Set a well-timed meeting to ask for a raise.** Don't blurt out, "I want a raise," as your boss is walking into the elevator or putting a bite of food in her mouth. Make an appointment for a sit-down meeting. Think about when your work might have deadlines that will stress out your boss. A good rule of thumb is not to ask for anything from a busy person first thing on a Monday morning. (Also avoid asking last thing on Friday, when she's trying to clear her desk and get out of there.)

17 **When you ask for a raise, don't compare yourself to other people.** You may have been inspired to ask for a raise when you realized that Lazy Frank, who is always taking off early, is making twice what you are, but don't bring it up. The issue is not that Lazy Frank is paid more than he is worth, but that *you* are worth more than *you* are being paid.

18 **Find out the going rate for your job description at other companies.** Come up with a well-researched figure that you think is fair, and then plan to ask for about 2 percent more. This will give your boss a bit of wiggle room for the negotiation.

19 **Write your own performance review before asking for a raise.** Lay out how your position has grown since you started working. List your major accomplishments and how they benefitted the company. Give concrete examples. Go over it in your head. You might even take a copy on paper to share with the boss when you make your pitch, especially if she has people above her she'll have to answer to—your review could help her make your case for you.

20 **Make sure your boss is sitting down when you ask for a raise.** Psychological studies have shown that your chances of persuading another person are enhanced if she is sitting down or reclining rather than standing. It doesn't matter as much whether you are sitting or standing.

21 **Make your pitch for a raise about them, not you.** You get a raise based on the good job you're doing, so focus on what you do for the company, not what you need from the company. Don't go in and talk about how your mortgage payment is always late and your kids need braces. That's not your boss's problem, even if he or she can sympathize.

22 **Give your boss a chance to make an offer.** Before you blurt out your figure, explain that you feel it's time for a raise, and see what your boss offers. She might surprise you with a figure higher than what you were ready to propose.

23 **Be prepared to take no for an answer.** Don't take it personally if your request for a raise is denied. The company may be in the middle of a budget freeze, and it may be beyond your boss's power to grant your request at this time. If you do get a no, ask if there might be some other form of reward for your effort—something that might make you happy in the short term. There may not be much that your boss can do, but if she values your contributions, she'll most likely try to come up with something to keep you happy.

24 **Don't make empty threats about your future with your workplace.** Don't threaten to quit or say you have another offer unless you actually do. Your boss might just call your bluff.

25 **Once you've made your case for a raise, ask for it—then stop talking.** People often get nervous at this point, and keep chattering away until they've talked themselves right out of a raise. Be confident, and let the silence work for you.

26 **Always back up your work.** In the old days, backing up data was a tedious process involving floppy discs and tape drives. Now there are external hard drives and online storage services that can back up everything automatically. Plugging an external hard drive into a computer's USB port is a quick and painless way to make sure you have another copy of your important data. Combine this with a software program that performs this task on a regular basis, and you're good to go.

27 **Save documents manually from time to time.** Even if you have a regular backup, take the extra step of saving the document manually every once in a while as you go. There are too many ways you can accidentally lose access to your data before your backup software has a chance to save it.

28 **Don't let your backup die with your computer.** Having an external hard drive next to your computer is great for hard-drive crashes, but it won't do you much good in the case of a fire or other natural disaster that destroys everything in the room. To be sure you still have your most important files after an emergency, back your files up to the cloud—i.e., the internet. You can do this by subscribing to an online service that lets you load files to their server. There are many companies that offer free storage for up to a certain amount of data, and will store larger amounts for a fee. Not only does this keep your data somewhere other than your house, but it also allows you to access it from different devices.

29 **Don't count on digital storage media to last forever.** No such perpetual storage medium has been invented. External drives burn out, and web-hosting sites suffer their own glitches or go out of business. Your best bet is to back up in a few places. Make more than one archive copy of your files, check the discs periodically to make sure they still work, and remember to re-archive your old data from time to time.

30 **Don't compress your data.** Even though most backup programs give you the option to compress data, it's a bad idea. To begin with, most photo and music files are already compressed, so you won't save much space. More importantly, if your files are compressed, you'll need to use the same program to restore and back them up. If the program becomes outmoded, or you lose access to it for some reason, your data could become unusable.

31 **Learn to spot fraudulent emails.** The best way to tell if an email is a fraud is to look at the address it's coming from. If it looks like it's supposed to be from eBay, but the email address is something like noreply@ebay.tz or mail1@eday.co, it's probably a scam. The safest thing to do is close the email and go directly to the site (eBay, in this case) by typing in the URL. From there, you can log in to your account and see if there are in fact any fabulous deals or compromises in security that need your attention.

32 **Spot a computer virus.** Modern viruses can block your antivirus program, yet make it appear as if everything is fine. If your computer seems to be running more slowly than usual, or your hard drive is constantly spinning when you're not running any special programs, take it as a warning sign. If your internet connection becomes noticeably slower, it could also be a sign that something is wrong.

33 **Get a good antivirus program, but don't stop there.** It is important to update all of your programs—including your antivirus software— with the latest security patches. This can be time-consuming, but it is much less a bother than having to reformat and reinstall your entire operating system after a stubborn malware attack, or having to deal with all of the repercussions if your identity gets stolen.

34 **Don't use one password for everything.** If you do this, and a hacker steals your Facebook password, then he can use it to access your bank account.

35 **Don't choose a simple or lame password.** After analyzing data from cases in which systems were hacked and passwords were published, a security firm was able to make a list of the most common passwords. For your edification, here are the top ten—if you use one of these, you're inviting hackers to peek at your data: (1) password; (2) 123456; (3) 12345678; (4) 1234; (5) qwerty; (6) 12345; (7) dragon; (8) *too dirty to print here!*; (9) baseball; (10) football.

36 **Use succinct, specific email subject lines.** This makes everyone's life easier. A good example would be, "Subject: Questions about page six of

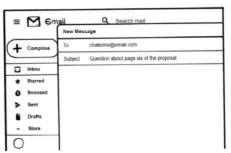

the proposal." A bad example would be, "Subject: Can you look this over?" (Even that, though, is preferable to "Subject: RE: re: re: Surfing cat video.")

37 **Don't say things in email that you don't want in writing.** You really don't want a record of anything that is embarrassing, offensive, unprofessional, or just plain mean. You can missend it, IT's filters may flag it, or you might accidentally leave it up on your screen when you run off to a meeting. Also, remember that the person you're emailing has a Forward button—and you may have forgotten her birthday last week.

38 **Don't email things that can be easily misconstrued.** Remember that email interactions don't include most of the visual cues of face-to-face communication. Jokes, for example, can be easily misinterpreted. Before you write, think about how your message could sound to someone who doesn't know your emotional state, or who doesn't have all the context that you have. Read it the way you would if you were angry—if it can be misconstrued, or you have to rely on emoticons to convey the right tone, you probably need to rethink and rewrite your message.

MONEY

1 **Keep a good credit score.** You don't need to carry a balance on your credit cards to have a good credit score, but you do need to have open lines of credit—and use them. If you know you have a problem keeping credit cards without overspending, this is one area where it's wise to consider whether your focus should be on your credit score or on your spending habits.

2 **Don't fall for companies that charge a fee for subscription credit-monitoring services.** The Fair Credit Reporting Act requires each of the nationwide consumer reporting companies to provide you with a free copy of your credit report at your request, once every twelve months or if you are turned down for a loan or line of credit. The Federal Trade Commission's website has information on how to make a request.

3 **Don't make late payments.** Besides leaving you with too much debt, this is the easiest way to screw up your credit score. To avoid this, consider consolidating your due dates so you never forget. Many companies let you change your billing cycle. Even seemingly trivial bills such as unpaid library fines or parking tickets can screw up your credit score if they end up going to collections.

4 **Boost your credit score by focusing on paying the right things.** Paying off installment loans—such as a car loan or a mortgage—does help your score, but not as much as paying down your credit cards. Ideally, to have a great credit score, you'd have a couple of credit cards that you've kept open for years and use regularly, but never get near your credit limit on them. This is why it's a bad idea to close your credit-card accounts: Even if you don't use the card, the ratio of presumably available credit to debt remains high. Lenders like this. You can also improve your scores by limiting your use of active accounts to less than 30 percent of the credit limit, whether you pay off the balance in full each month or not.

5 **When it comes to money, stay boring.** Research shows that most investors get a much better return with so called "low-volatility" stocks: those subject to only modest price fluctuations. Over the past decade, the 100 least volatile stocks in the Standard and Poor's 500 index outperformed the overall index by 67 percentage points. Slow and steady wins the race!

6 **Don't bother with hot stocks.** By the time a stock gets really hot, it's probably too late. By that time, there's often little advantage left to putting money into it. A corollary to this advice: don't follow the news too closely. Investors are often swayed by the big story in the headlines. An accident at a power plant might lead them to sell off energy stocks, for example, even though the crisis is temporary and manageable. A big story on a hot new offering can create similarly unrealistic hype.

7 **Look for good ignored stocks.** When you see all of the investors going in one direction, look for gems among the companies they're ignoring. Even if an otherwise sound company has had recent problems, it's probably a safe bet if it has good management, a healthy market share, a history of earnings growth, and low debt. More important than the events of the day are the long-term trends.

8 **Avoid stocks that try to rally and fail to make a new high.** These are most likely duds. If you look at a stock chart and see that a stock's highs are not as high as they used to be and the lows are dipping deeper, that's a sign that the stock is trending down. Don't hold out for the next big rally.

9 **Know your investing weaknesses.** If you can't tear yourself away from the financial news, and you know you have a tendency to react emotionally to everything you hear, make a vow to sell only when the stock market is closed. That way, you won't be swayed by every little fluctuation.

10 **Use protective stop orders with your broker.** These instruct your broker to sell your stock automatically when it drops below a certain point. As the stock rises, you can cancel an old stop order and enter a new one.

11 **Don't let your emotions cloud your investment judgment.** Studies show that people are more influenced by the fear of loss than by dreams of gain. Keep this tendency in mind whenever you find yourself holding onto shares long after you should have sold them. Look over the pattern of your trades and see if there are certain times of the year when you seem to be more reluctant to sell. You may discover that the anniversary of a painful event, such as the loss of a loved one, has been subconsciously prodding you to avoid loss at that time.

12 **Protect your important ID numbers carefully.** Guard your social security number, credit card numbers, and driver's license especially closely. These are the keystones that an ID thief can build upon. Be especially protective of your PIN numbers, and never write them on your ATM cards or on anything you keep in your wallet with the cards.

13 **Before you use an ATM, look at it closely.** Technologically savvy felons sometimes create skimming devices that fit over the card reader at an ATM to read the magnetic stripe on a card before it enters the real machine. This is combined with a camera that records time-stamped footage of victims punching in their PIN numbers, so that the scammers can match up the information later on. (When in doubt, your best defense against such cameras is to cover your hand when entering your PIN.)

14 **Shred bank and credit statements, as well as mailed credit-card offers.** A thief can take these out of the garbage and sign up for the offers in your name. If you suddenly stop receiving mail, call the post office. Sometimes a crook will forge your signature and have your mail forwarded somewhere else in order to obtain information or hide evidence of identity appropriation.

15 **Never give out personal information in response to an email or a call that you didn't initiate.** Scammers will sometimes pretend to be from entities with which you do legitimate business. If you receive an email that says there's a problem with your PayPal account, for example, and you're worried that it may be true, don't follow the link in the message. Instead, log in to your account as you normally would. If there's a real problem with your account, you should have some kind of notification besides the email.

16 **Check your credit report at least once a year.** This will tip you off to any credit lines that were opened in your name. If you discover anything out of the ordinary, put a fraud alert in your credit file by contacting the credit bureaus. When you've done that, any future credit application will have to be confirmed with you over the phone.

17 **Keep high-tuition colleges on your list.** One mistake that many people with lower incomes make is to not even consider high-tuition colleges. If you have the grades, don't shy away from an Ivy League school. Because of their loyal alumni, they often have large endowments to aid promising students, and if you qualify for need-based aid, you might end up paying less at a top-rated school than at a state school where aid is more limited.

18 **Always apply for tuition aid.** There is no real income cutoff for tuition aid—but you definitely won't qualify if you don't apply. Even if you're a perfect candidate for financial aid, you won't get it if you miss the deadlines. Don't wait until an acceptance letter rolls in. Apply for aid at the same time you file your application to attend.

19 **Try to pay in-state tuition.** You may be able to pay in-state tuition while attending an out-of-state institution. More than half of states provide reduced-tuition programs for students from certain neighboring states when the program they want isn't offered in their home state. For more information, look up the New England Regional Student Program, the Midwestern Higher

Education Compact, the Southern Regional Education Board, or the Western Interstate Commission for Higher Education.

20 **Look into unusual scholarships.** You may be surprised by the variety of scholarships, savings plans, and tuition-savings programs out there. There are scholarships especially for Star Trek fans, for students who have worked as golf caddies, for champion marbles players, and for people with an academic interest in sheep. A college-tuition aid expert studies all of your financial options full-time. Take advantage of his or her expertise.

21 **If you can, stay with your job for a few extra years.** Don't retire just because you're offered an early retirement package that sounds

appealing. Stick to your plan. Not only does working longer allow you to put money away instead of drawing it out, but the amount of Social Security benefits you receive also increases by about 8 percent each year.

22 **Gather a nest egg that will last.** Plan as if you're going to live to be 95 to be sure you don't outlast your retirement funds. Keep your annual drawdown rate to 4 percent of assets—at that rate, if you start withdrawing at age 65, you'll have a cash flow until age 95.

23 **Remember: A career is about more than just money.** If you love your job and you're not sure you're ready to stop working, then don't. Even if you're ready to stop punching in each day, think about the nonfinancial benefits working gives you. Then make a plan to address some of what you'll be giving up. You may discover that there's only so much leisure you can handle!

24 **Make yourself a will—now.** The biggest mistake people make when it comes to a will is not having one at all. Sure, you're young and not planning to die anytime soon—but who is? Don't wait for "the right time." If you die intestate—meaning without a will—all your assets will be distributed under state law. That may or may not be where you would want them to go.

25 **Don't hide your will.** Sometimes people hide their wills away because they don't want relatives to take a peek and learn what they will or won't be getting until it's time. The problem is, if you hide it so well that no one knows about it, it's the same as not having one.

26 **Give the executor of your will a heads-up.** This person will be responsible for handling the transfer of all your assets, which is a big responsibility. Be sure you have chosen someone who is willing and able to do it, and let them know that you've named them executor.

27 **Don't assume your will takes care of everything.** There are some assets a will does not cover—for example, your IRA. The person you name as the beneficiary in your IRA documents will receive those funds, regardless of what your will says. The same is true of many insurance policies. Property that's held jointly will go to the

surviving co-owner, even if you name someone else as a beneficiary in your will.

28 **Don't assume there won't be disputes over your estate.** Just because you don't have a fortune doesn't mean everything will be easily resolved. If your will states that your personal items are to be "divided equally" among your children, it won't keep them from fighting over a particular heirloom. A much better strategy is to ask them what objects they value while you're still alive, and then either give them the items before you die, or list each item specifically in the will with explanations as to why you've given what to whom.

29 **Consider setting up a trust instead of using a will.** Everything listed in your will must pass through probate, which can be expensive and time-consuming. Instead of transferring all your property through your will, you might want to set up various trusts, which can reduce your tax burden and bypass the probate process.

30 **Know your funerary options.** No state requires the embalming of a body. The least expensive funerary option is usually a "direct burial" or "direct cremation," in which the body is buried or cremated shortly after death with no formal service by the funeral home. A memorial service can be held later. If you don't plan to have a viewing, you don't need to pay for dressing the body or cosmetics. It's also legal to bury a body in something other than a traditional casket—some religious traditions even require a body to be interred in a shroud or plain pine box.

31 **Purchase a casket directly from the manufacturer.** For families struggling to cover the costs of a funeral, this can help. Many sites on the internet will allow you to comparison-shop and have the casket shipped overnight for a fee.

32 **Don't list your burial and funeral instructions in your will.** Most wills aren't read for some time after a person has died, and you'll probably be in the ground before that happens. (This is also true of safety-deposit boxes belonging to a deceased person, which are sealed by banks until legal proceedings have taken place.) If you have specific funeral wishes, use a separate document to detail them, and be sure your family knows about whatever arrangements you may already have made—or you may end up paying twice for your own funeral!

MEDICAL CARE

1 **Read original medical journal articles in full.** If a story cites research that is particularly relevant to you—for example, about a medication that you take—look up the original journal article. It'll tell you more than an article in the popular press. If you can't find the original article online, you may be able to get a copy at your local library.

2 **Talk to your doctor about anything you read that scares you.** All medications have side effects, for example, and taking them requires an analysis of the risks of taking the medication versus the dangers of not taking it. Your physician should be able to explain why he thinks the benefits outweigh the risks in your case, and put your mind at ease about it.

3 **Look into sellers' credentials before using their health products or services.** If someone is trying to sell you something, confirm his or her health claims with an outside source. An expert on germs whose research is funded by a bleach manufacturer may have a vested interest in reporting that bleach is the best cleaning solution. If your favorite television doctor's program is full of sponsored product placements, you are smart to question whether the product is being recommended for health or business reasons.

4 **Tell your healthcare provider if you don't have insurance.** They will often be able to negotiate a lower price for you. Bear in mind that insurance companies typically pay doctors one-half to two-thirds of the amount billed. Your doctor usually has the wiggle room to cut you some slack. Your doctor may also be willing to waive or reduce the fee for your follow-up visit, if it's just to share results and will only take a few moments.

5 Consider getting routine tests done directly at a lab rather than at the doctor's office. When your doctor does a test, she charges you for the visit and a fee for drawing your blood, plus whatever the lab charges to run the test. Instead, ask your doctor to send you the necessary paperwork and then go online and look for clinical, medical, and diagnostics laboratories in your area.

6 If you have a prescription that you can't afford, look up the drug manufacturer's web page. Most pharmaceutical companies have programs that provide free drugs to people who qualify. Different programs have different criteria, and you may well fit them.

7 Visit a mini-clinic for basic treatments. Many grocery stores and drugstores are equipped with mini-clinics that can handle basic procedures. Going there for treatment of minor health problems like bronchitis and rashes can save you a substantial amount, compared to a full-service doctor visit.

8 **Save money by visiting a federally funded health center.** The U.S. Department of Health and Human Services maintains a list of federally funded health centers that will care for you, even if you have no health insurance. There, you pay what you can afford, based on your income. Search for a center near you at http://findahealthcenter.hrsa.gov.

9 **Double-check that all medical tests are necessary.** Doctors may advocate for doing tests just to be sure that all bases are covered. If you're looking for ways to conserve money or simply don't want the invasiveness of so many tests, ask your doctor which ones are vital versus optional, or seek a second opinion.

10 **Ask for itemized hospital bills.** When you are admitted to the hospital, tell a staff member that you want an itemized bill brought to you each day.

Hospitals are required to do this if you ask. If you see that you were billed for two doctor visits and you only remember receiving one, ask to speak to the hospital's patient advocate and ask him to explain any charges you don't understand.

11 **Keep a sharp lookout for double billings at hospitals.** Hospitals often bill patients twice for the same thing. For example, if you're billed for scrubs and gloves worn by the surgical staff, ask your advocate if this is also covered under costs for operating-room time.

12 **Expect not to pay for the last day of your hospital stay.** Hospital patients are charged the full day's room rate for the day they check in, even if they arrived at 11:30 p.m. The trade-off is that they are not supposed to be charged for the last day. Hospitals often forget this and charge for the last day anyway.

13 **Don't get billed for an extra day.** If the hospital tells you that you won't be charged if you're out by noon, ask your doctor if she can give you your final checkup in the morning so you can be out before then. If she can't, clarify with your nurse or physician assistant that you shouldn't be charged because the late checkout was your doctor's doing. Don't be afraid to request more information from the hospital's billing specialist.

14 **If you feel you were overbilled at a hospital, hire an independent medical-billing advocate.** They charge a fee for their services, either per hour or as a percentage of the amount saved. The former will probably save you money, and the latter definitely will.

15 **Don't avoid giving healthcare instructions to loved ones.** As unpleasant as it is to contemplate, you should draft a healthcare proxy that will name someone to make medical decisions for you in the event that you are unable to do so yourself. Include end-of-life directives that lay out what types of medical life support you wish to receive in case of a terminal illness. This can relieve some of the burden on your family that comes with making these hard choices.

WELLNESS

1   **Always remove splinters.** It's a myth that splinters will work their way out themselves—they should always be removed. If you don't remove them, they will likely become infected in a day or two.

2   **Let difficult splinters scab over.** If you can't get a splinter out after twenty minutes or so, stop jabbing at it, wash the area thoroughly, and wait until the splinter is covered with scab tissue. Then you can remove both the splinter and the scab together. If you still aren't able to remove the splinter after 48 to 72 hours, or you begin to experience swelling or redness, it's time to visit the doctor.

3 **Try steaming out a splinter.** Fill a glass or wide-mouthed bottle three-fourths full of hot water. Then place the skin with the splinter over the mouth and press down slightly. The steam will soften the skin around the splinter, and if the splinter is wood, the steam will cause the wood to expand, which might allow it to pop out on its own.

4 **Don't specifically avoid spicy foods if you're worried about an ulcer.** You can't give yourself an ulcer by eating spicy foods, nor can you cure one by eating bland foods or drinking milk. Any food—spicy or bland—stimulates the production of ulcer-exacerbating stomach acids.

5 **Eat the right food to end intestinal distress.** A bland diet of bananas, rice, apples, and toast puts soluble fiber in your system and slows the passage of food through the intestinal tract, which can help with digestive trouble. Be sure to get enough fluids, too.

6 **When you have diarrhea, be careful not to get dehydrated.** Drink plenty of fluids to make up for what you're losing. If your diarrhea lasts for more than seventy-two hours, if it's accompanied by abdominal pain, or if it's accompanied by a high fever or dizziness, seek medical attention.

7 **Properly treat a black eye.** The best way to treat a shiner is to sit down, tilt your head back, and apply a plain ice bag wrapped in cloth. The cold should be applied for five minutes, then taken off for five minutes before repeating. If you want to take something for the pain, try a pain reliever such as acetaminophen instead of aspirin—aspirin reduces blood clotting, which can make a bruise worse. Once the injury has turned blue, the only thing that will heal it is time, although continuing to apply cold will help reduce swelling.

8 **Only use crutches if you can use them safely.** One problem with crutches is that people who should really be using a walker sometimes refuse to do so because they think it makes them appear weak or old. No matter your age, use a walker or wheelchair when you need greater support for strength, stability, and balance, such as after a hip or knee surgery.

9 **Slow down on crutches.** Don't expect to get around on crutches as quickly as you do without them. Take it slowly; as you practice, your balance and coordination will improve.

10 **Don't try to get too fit too fast.** As tempted as you may be to throw yourself head-first into a new exercise routine in response to a doctor's advice or perhaps as a New Year's resolution, take your time. Jump in too quickly and you'll risk getting hurt instead: pulled muscles, injured backs, overexertion, and accidents are the usual results.

11 **Use a spotter whenever you lift weights.** This is true whether you're lifting at home or at the gym. If a certain lift hurts, try substituting another movement that works the same body part from a different angle. If your gym offers a free personal-training session, take it so you can learn how to use all the weights and equipment properly.

12 **Know when the workout pain you're feeling is the wrong kind.** There's a difference between feeling your muscles burn from working them out properly and feeling straight-up pain. When you start to hurt, rest—even if it's a muscle burn that doesn't indicate injury. Real, non-workout-ache pain is your body's way of saying that you've gone too far. If you're feeling it, you're either doing something that's too advanced for you, or doing something that you shouldn't be doing at all. Just try to increase your activity a little bit each week until you reach your goal.

13 **Drink plenty of water while you work out.**
Anyone who ever told you that you shouldn't drink liquids while exercising was wrong. If you don't replace the fluids that you lose by sweating, you're at risk of dehydration and heat stroke. Don't wait until you're thirsty to drink—by then you're already dehydrated, and exercise can blunt your body's thirst signals. A good rule of thumb is to drink two cups of water fifteen minutes before you start exercising, and about a half a cup of water every ten to fifteen minutes while working out.

14 **Never drink alcohol on an empty stomach.**
When you have nothing but alcohol in your system, it's absorbed rapidly by the small intestine. You'll end up yacking up later on. Eating after you're already drunk doesn't help nearly as much as eating beforehand.

15 **Avoid dehydration to avoid a hangover.** Most of the herbal concoctions and tablets that claim to fight hangovers seem to work only because you take them with plenty of water. The smarter thing to do is to start drinking water before you even pick up that cocktail. Then alternate each alcoholic drink with a glass of water.

16 **Know how to cure a hangover.** Drink a lot of water or an electrolyte solution (such as Gatorade) to reverse your dehydration. Even though you may not feel like it, eat a well-balanced breakfast too. Alcohol raises your insulin levels, which can make you feel weak and tired; eating will raise your glucose levels. Coffee will just increase your dehydration and make your hangover more wide-awake, so avoid it. You might also try taking a vitamin and mineral supplement—as the alcohol was busy dehydrating you with extra trips to the lavatory, it was also washing away whatever vitamins you had going in your system. For your headache, take ibuprofen—but *not* acetaminophen. You may still have alcohol in your system, and acetaminophen combined with alcohol can cause liver damage.

17 **Try to avoid the combination of tobacco and alcohol.** If it seems that smoking makes you want to drink more, and drinking makes you want to smoke more, it's because they do. Alcohol makes your veins expand and nicotine makes them contract, so as your body attempts to even out these effects, the one makes you crave the other.

18 **If you think you might be having a heart attack, don't panic.** Easier said than done—but fear will only make your heart race more and use up more oxygen, which, if you are having a heart attack, is already in limited circulation. Instead, stop everything. Don't try to find a place to sit; just lie down on the ground with your legs elevated to keep as much blood pooled around your heart as possible, and think calming thoughts. If you have a watch with a second hand, focus on the second hand. For each second, think (or quietly say), "Heartbeat." Repeat. Breathe. This will increase oxygen delivery to the heart.

19 **Tell someone if you think you're having a heart attack.** Ask him to call an ambulance, even if you're not sure. Who cares if you're wrong? No matter what's actually happening, something is obviously going haywire, and you need immediate assistance. If it turns out not to be anything serious, good. This is absolutely a time to be safe rather than sorry.

20 **Take aspirin ASAP during a heart attack.** Take one 325-mg aspirin tablet, or four 81-mg baby aspirins. Heart attacks are caused by clogged spots in the blood vessels that supply oxygen to the heart muscle. Aspirin doesn't remove those blockages, but it does keep blood from clotting and adding to them. If you have adult rather than children's aspirin, don't swallow it whole—it'll take too long to take effect. Chew it up.

21 **Increase oxygen in the room during a heart attack.** Assuming you don't have an oxygen mask handy, have someone open the windows to increase the room's oxygen level. Coughing can help keep you from fainting and keep you conscious until someone can administer CPR. Breathe, then cough, every three seconds. Take a breath in through your nose, think "heartbeat, heartbeat, heartbeat," and then cough as an exhale.

22 **When feeling faint, lie down on a bed, couch, or even the floor.** It should only take a minute or two for your dizziness to pass. If the faint feeling goes on longer than that, seek immediate medical attention.

23 **Don't try to revive a passed-out person by splashing water on his face.** A person who is unconscious cannot control his throat muscles, and he could choke on anything that goes into his throat. You can gently apply cool water to the person's face, but don't throw it at him.

24 **Don't give alcohol to an unconscious person.** You've probably seen a number of flicks in which some passed-out person is revived with booze. Usually a grubby antihero pours a little mystery alcohol into the injured party's mouth from a flask that no one is surprised they have. Then the person comes to. Not only is this a myth, but the alcohol method is bad all around. In addition to presenting a swallowing danger, giving an unconscious person alcohol lowers his or her blood pressure, which can make a fainting spell worse.

SOCIAL LIFE

1 **Make sure your smile conveys openness and warmth.** It's got to be the right kind of smile—if you immediately jump to a full-on grin, you'll come across like a salesperson, not a potential friend. Instead, you want to give a "slow-flooding" smile—a smile that builds slowly.

2 **When you first meet someone, pay attention to eye color.** While you're noticing a person's eye color, you must gaze into her eyes, which will make you seem trustworthy. Poor eye contact will make you seem dishonest. Don't carry the noticing thing too far, though—if you stare too long, you'll make the other person uncomfortable.

3 **Stand up when you meet someone new.**
You may have heard that men should stand for greetings, while women should remain sitting. Forget that. Regardless of gender, anyone who is able should stand up and make eye contact. If you're in a booth at a restaurant and can't get up, extend your hand and say something like, "Excuse me for not standing. Pleased to meet you."

4 **Use open body language when meeting someone.** Keep your arms uncrossed and your hands unclenched. Point your heart toward the heart of the other person.

5 **Mirror a person's gestures and body language to put them at ease.** People are more apt to like a person whom they perceive as similar to themselves. If your new friend talks with her hands, do the same. If she speaks softly, speak softly. If she laughs a lot, laugh a lot. After a few moments of matching, try changing your movements. If the other person follows suit, it shows that she feels in sync with you.

6 **Train your mind to remember names.** The more important you consider names to be, the easier you will find them to remember. Repeat someone's name as soon as you meet them: "It's nice to meet you, Mike." Then use the name frequently in conversation: "What a coincidence, Mike! I was at the same concert." Remember back in school when teachers had you repeat times tables by rote to memorize them? The same idea applies here. Repetition helps you remember.

7 **To remember a name, focus on a prominent feature.** Don't worry about whether or not the feature you choose is flattering—you don't need to share it, you just need to remember it. If Wanda is the one with the wrinkles, think, *Wanda-wrinkles*. The sillier and more creative you are with this technique, the more likely you'll be to remember. And if the person's name has another meaning, you're in luck! Picture Bob bobbing in the water, or Joy laughing, or Jack propping up a car on a jack.

8 **Introduce yourself if it seems you need to.** If you get the feeling that someone who's introducing you can't remember your name, do him a favor and say your name before he has to ask. Extend your hand and say, "Hi, I'm [your name]." The person introducing you will remember your kindness. You can also help a new acquaintance remember your name by dropping it again later in the conversation.

9 **Add some expression to your phone voice.** It's easy to come across as a bit low on energy over the telephone, even when you speak in your normal voice. The other caller can't see your face, which means he loses a lot of emotional cues. To make up for this, you should add about 30 percent more expressiveness to your voice than you would use face-to-face. It may seem a bit unnatural at first, but it will sound normal to the other caller.

10 **Use a simple trick to make a caller feel important.** Speak with a normal energy level when you first pick up the phone, then shift into your high-energy telephone voice after the other person has given her name: *"Ellen!* Glad to hear from you!" The person on the other end of the phone will have warmer feelings toward you when she senses you're pleased to speak to her.

11 **Use your speaking partner's name more frequently than usual over the phone.** People love to hear their own names, and you'll seem more engaged and energetic if you use the other person's name a bit more than you might face-to-face.

12 **Consider how you'll handle leaving a message before you make a call.** Avoid stumbling through an awkward voicemail message, or the inverse awkward "Oh, I thought I was going to get the machine" moment, by preparing in advance for both possibilities. Have a voicemail message ready to recite, but also plan the opening of a conversation with a real live human being.

13 **Set up the end of your phone conversation early on.** At the beginning of you call, try to get an idea of what the other person was doing when you called. For example, you might ask, "Have I caught you at a bad time?" The other person might say, "Oh no, I was just reading a book." Then, when you're ready, you can end the conversation with, "OK, I'll let you get back to your book."

14 **Plan your call to keep it short.** Do you dread calling someone because you feel like you'll never get off the phone? Try to time the call just before he goes out to lunch or leaves the office. This will give him a reason to cut the conversation short.

15 **Remember to ignore the phone sometimes.** Just because the telephone is ringing doesn't mean you have to pick it up—that's why voicemail was invented! If you're in the middle of a project that requires all your attention, let the phone ring and call the person back when you're able to focus. (It's also perfectly legitimate to pick up and politely tell the caller that he has reached you at a bad time.) If you talk over the phone when you don't feel like it, you'll just sound distracted and unprepared.

16 **When passing an acquaintance, make eye contact at the right time.** You are generally expected to acknowledge a person you pass with eye contact at about the eight-foot mark (roughly two and a half meters). If the person coming your way is an acquaintance, you should look down and pretend not to have spotted her until you get to that magic distance. Otherwise, you'll have to contend with another gaffe: having to keep on recognizing the person with gestures, waves, and silly expressions for the entire, horrifying length of your walk.

17 **When passing a stranger, signal your route with a glance.** The eight-foot mark is where you negotiate passage. You do this by making eye contact, and then looking down to the path where you intend to walk. For this to work, the other person must pick up on the signal and move out of the way. If you glance at the wrong moment, you miss your partner's glance, or both signal the same direction and refuse to yield, you'll collide.

18 **Write down a good joke when you hear it.** In order to tell a joke, you have to remember it. The biggest joke disasters happen when you launch into your humorous tale only to discover that you haven't quite committed the pertinent details—the punch line, for example—to memory. As soon as you hear a joke that you might want to tell later, write it down.

19 **Tell a new joke frequently to commit it to memory.** Don't wait a year until you trot out your joke, or you'll never remember it. Tell it a few times after you first hear it, so that you can commit it to memory. Try to remember whom you have already told it to, too—jokes are funny largely due to the element of surprise. Your sister will be far less delighted by your joke on the eighth telling.

20 **Don't overtell a joke. Telling a joke is not like reenacting *The Barber of Seville*.** You need to be brief, upbeat, and to the point. Don't embellish. Get to the punch line in as few steps as possible, but be sure you don't leave any important bits out. Make eye contact with your listeners. Unless you're a natural comic or have a degree in theater, don't try to mime the action or perform accents and voices you aren't able to do.

21 **Don't oversell a joke, either.** Even a decent joke will have trouble getting a laugh if you've oversold it. Don't start by saying, "I heard the

funniest joke. You'll really laugh at this." You're setting the bar awfully high, and making it even harder for yourself to clear the hurdle by taking away part of the element of surprise. (That said, don't undersell a joke by apologizing in advance for it, or saying something like, "I heard this joke, but I don't know if it's funny or not. What do you think?" Just start telling it, and let your audience react as they will.)

22 **If you're repeating a joke you heard on TV, say so.** Don't pretend you wrote it, or that it happened to you. Otherwise you may be called out when one of your friends says, "That wasn't you, that was George Carlin! I saw it on YouTube."

23 **Approach apologies with the right attitude.** Apologizing involves swallowing your pride and admitting you're not perfect. Even though most people don't like doing this, there is no way around it. Remember: Your goal in an apology is not to save face, but to express your regret. Your apology should not be about your feelings, but about the feelings of the other person. Try to see the situation from their perspective, and use empathy to show you understand how your actions affected them.

24 **Don't give excuses while apologizing.** Your apology is going to fail, and rightly, if it contains more excuses and justifications than remorse. Of course there were reasons you behaved as you did. But if you ended up doing something that hurt someone else, they're probably not great reasons to begin with—and even if they are ("I was only racing to save a child from a burning building when I ran over your poodle"), now is not the time to bring them up.

25 **Accept full responsibility while apologizing.** Don't try to shift the blame; you'll end up sounding like one child pointing at another on the playground and saying, "He did it!" This is not actually an apology: "I'm sorry I made you cry, but if you hadn't gotten on my case like that, I wouldn't have called you that name." To apologize is to accept full responsibility for your actions—no ifs or buts.

26 **Resist the impulse to shift an apology into the second or third person.** This is a place where many apologies go wrong. When you say, "I'm sorry you didn't understand me," you're not apologizing for your actions; you're telling the other person that you're sorry he reacted the way he did. A real apology begins, "I'm sorry I . . ."

27 **For a real apology, actually say the words.** Don't try to get away with a "mistakes were made" statement. Say "I'm sorry" or "I apologize."

28 **Offer a solution to undo what you did.** Part of admitting you've acted wrongly is trying to make the situation right. "I'm sorry I broke your vase. Can I give you the money to replace it?" "I'm sorry I hurt your feelings. I'll work on my short temper so I don't do that again." "I'm sorry I forgot your birthday. Is there anything I can do to make it up to you?"

29 **Be sincere about changing your ways.** If this is the tenth time you've said, "I'm sorry I didn't call. I'll remember to do that next time," your apology will not be believed— nor should it be.

30 **Don't expect an apology to magically fix everything.** Especially if you've really screwed up, your apology may not work right away. Accept that it may take a while for you to receive the other person's forgiveness and trust. If the other person doesn't react the way you'd like, don't keep arguing the point. Simply say, "I understand. Again, I am sorry," and give them some time to cool down.

31 **When comforting a grieving friend, keep the focus on them.** Remember that each person's grief is unique. When the grief is new, don't say, "I know how you feel," or "That's just how I felt when my mother died." Don't offer advice. Think back to how you felt in the past and tap into what helped you—without using the words, "You know what helped me?"

32 **Be patient with your grieving friend.** Give them time to cry and to sit with their emotions; don't interrupt or rush to respond. Putting a hand on your friend's arm can be highly supportive, but don't rush to hug a person who starts to cry—it can be interpreted as an effort to stop the tears.

33 **Don't allow your discomfort with a friend's grief to make you a stranger.** It's easy to get caught up in worrying about saying the wrong thing. But even a clumsy effort will be appreciated more than leaving your friend alone with her grief.

34 **Maintain your friendships.** If your friends are what you truly value in life, then you need to put effort into maintaining them. You might, for example, block out a bit of time on your smartphone calendar marked "spending time with Betty."

35 **Treat friendship as a health need.** If you have trouble justifying taking time away from work and other commitments to spend with friends, try thinking of it as medical leave. We need to give and receive support in order to be happy and healthy. (Giving support is just as important to happiness as getting support.) If you have five or more close friends, you're far more

likely to describe yourself as "very happy." When seniors spend time with friends, they cut their odds of memory loss in half and are twice as likely to avoid disabilities.

36 **Stay in touch, even if only briefly.** If you really are unavoidably busy for a short period, a quick phone call or email exchange will do to stay in touch with a friend. If, on the other hand, you're constantly too busy to get together, your friend cannot be faulted for thinking you don't place a high priority on her friendship, and moving on.

37 **Don't alienate people with your sense of humor.** What you find funny may not translate well to everyone. The social media research company NM Incite did a study of friending and unfriending behavior. The top reason that people ended a social network relationship was that they were sick of seeing offensive posts. (Fifty-five percent of those surveyed said they had dropped a friend for that reason.)

38 **Don't make a commercial message out of every online status update.** It's OK to mention your new line of handbags on social media once in a while, but do it too often and you'll lose friends and followers. Instead, set up a page for your wares and update people through that. They'll be more receptive to something that's upfront.

39 **Don't be a constant downer online.** Some people turn to social networks as a place to vent frustrations and elicit sympathy. If you *only* post your complaints, however, you're likely to add social rejection to your long list of problems. Twenty percent of the respondents in an NM Incite poll said they had unfriended someone because their posts were too depressing.

40 **Don't get upset about being "unfriended" online.** Bear in mind that many of your contacts are probably not "friends" in any real sense of the word. If you find that your college roommate's friend, whom you met twice twenty years ago, has decided she doesn't need to keep up with your day-to-day activities, try not to take it personally.

41 **Smile for the camera.** Study after study has shown that people rate others as more attractive when they smile, so whenever you're having your picture taken, do it. The trick is to have a genuine smile—people can sense the difference, even in photographs. If the camera seems to capture a true moment of joy in you, people will love the way you look. So relax when the camera comes out, and give in to the fun you're already having.

42 **Don't stress about your looks in photos.** Your fear of looking bad can become a self-fulfilling prophecy! Relax your face and your mind; think about something funny. A great photo is full of motion and action. Instead of standing in a stiff pose, do something silly. You don't want the statue you're standing beside to appear livelier than you!

DATING AND RELATIONSHIPS

1 **Don't talk yourself out of asking someone out.** You may not have to have a lot of money for a first date, but you have just enough imagination to choose something fun and interesting. A bike ride can be a great way to spend time with a person (and it even gets the heart pumping a bit, which might just increase their attraction to you—see #6).

2 **Don't waste time rehearsing an opening line.** Magazines like to run stories on terrible pickup lines because they're entertaining, not because they make or break your chances for a relationship. The first impression you create has much more to do with your demeanor and your tone than what you say. It's more important to use good timing than to say something memorable.

(Good timing, by the way, is before your potential new partner gets away!)

3 **When asking someone out, use relaxed body language.** You want body language that conveys that you're a nice person and not an ax murderer. Make eye contact, smile, and speak more slowly than your normal pace. This gives the other person time to switch their focus to you and gives you more time to think. Remember, your goal is to get a conversation going. Present an upturned palm mid-conversation or shrug your shoulders. This says, "I'm harmless."

4 **Don't pretend to be outgoing if you aren't.** Asking someone out doesn't mean you have to pretend to be anything. Nor should you play hard to get. (The object of your desire might interpret this as lack of interest.) If your goal is to meet someone you're compatible with over the long haul, you need to pair up with someone who likes your *real* personality.

5 **Be prepared for rejection.** Sad but true, the person you want may not feel the same spark. Not all risks end in reward (or they wouldn't be risks!).

Feel good about yourself for taking that shot—
hopefully you'll have better luck next time.

6 **For an exciting first date, do something active.** If you really want to be attractive to your potential partner on a first date, get his or her blood pumping. Go dancing. Ride a roller coaster. Go biking. Try climbing a rock wall. All of these things get the heart racing, which is just what you want. Your date will subconsciously connect that excitement with you. Psychologists call it "misattribution of arousal," but you can call it "awesome."

7 **If you're looking for a low-pressure first date, meet for coffee.** This is a great first date: it's economical and nonthreatening, and if you choose a coffee shop near another attraction, you can go on from the coffee shop to another activity if you're really enjoying each other's company.

What's more, coffee is a stimulant that gets the heart pumping while at the same time allowing for an in-depth, getting-to-know-you conversation.

8 **Follow body language cues during a date.** To start with, know the difference between a polite smile and the real thing. If your date is happy to be with you, the corners of her eyes will be squinting. Depending on her age, you may see crow's feet. If the smile hasn't reached the eyes, it's probably plastered on for your benefit. You can also check interest with a quick glance at the feet. If your date's toes are pointed in your direction, that's good. If they're pointed in another direction, it means she's planning her escape route.

9 **Know the implications of flowers and gifts.** Early in your courtship you may want to buy flowers and gifts to win your beloved's favor, and it's not a bad thing to do. Studies show that giving a gift makes you feel more committed to the recipient and improves your self-esteem. The effects on the recipient can be much more mixed, however. Receiving a gift might make someone happy, or it might lead to negative feelings of pressure to commit.

10 **Plant the seeds conversationally for long-term love.** If your goal is something more than a quick fling, you can convey that with your conversation. You don't need to talk about marriage and babies—in fact, doing so is almost guaranteed to cause panic in a first date. Thoughts of love relate to an abstract future, so ask about abstractions and the future. What are your date's dreams and goals? What's his or her philosophy of life? Ask "why" instead of "what."

11 **To keep a relationship strong, keep kissing.** Foster closeness with your partner by kissing often, without treating sex as the ultimate goal. Couples who engage in more nonsexual kissing report greater relationship intimacy and less stress.

12 **Elicit lustful thoughts on a date by keeping conversation focused on specific present things.** Lust is about the here and now. You can prime your date to think in these terms by adjusting what psychologists call the "construal level" of the experience—the mental closeness of the things you're experiencing together. Talk about recent past activities, what excites your date now, and how things in the current environment taste, feel, smell, and look.

13 **Don't project your own tastes and desires onto the object of your desire.** Your partner is different from you and likes different things—which is, after all, part of the attraction. This means there will have to be some empathy, imagination, and compromise at work to make sparks fly.

14 **Kiss the way your partner wants.** If you ask women what the biggest kissing error is, they will tell you that it is an overly enthusiastic tongue. Men, on the other hand, are more likely to say that the biggest mistake women make is not opening their mouths wide enough. These two facts taken together paint a clear picture: He wants a passionate French kiss, and she wants him to rein in his tongue activity. Generally speaking, a woman's area of kissing pleasure is more diffuse than a man's—many women love to be kissed on the neck and ears, not just the lips, so a combination of soft lip and tongue kisses and kisses on the neck will produce the most satisfying results for a woman. Men often find this hard to believe, because the same kisses do nothing for them. On the other hand, a woman who loves to be kissed on the neck will assume her male partner loves it just as much as she does—and while she's kissing his neck with gusto, his lips are getting cold, and he's getting bored.

15 **Don't be in a rush to get married.** If you conclude that any of your partner's habits are red flags, you should wait to marry, or you might need to call it off entirely—and this is true even if you've already announced your engagement. Once the momentum of wedding plans gets going, it can seem almost impossible to stop. But it isn't. If you realize things aren't right at this point, calling it off won't be pleasant—but will the divorce process be any more pleasant?

16 **Tell friends and family right away about a called-off engagement.** You don't want them to find out when you change your Facebook status from "engaged" to "single." You do not need to give them any lengthy explanation—just say that you've decided not to marry at this time. If you've already sent out wedding invitations, you'll have to send out a second card announcing that the ceremony has been canceled. Again, don't feel that you need to include any particulars. (And yes, you do have to return any gifts you've gotten.)

17 **Keep divorce proceedings amicable.**
No matter how bad things get, you're both still people who at one point could stand each other. Keep that in mind. Don't let a divorce lawyer steer your negotiations. Before you make your first call to a lawyer, you should sit down as rational people and see what arrangements you can agree on. The more you can work out now, the less complicated (and less expensive) it will all be later.

18 **Don't get hung up on who's getting the better deal in your divorce.** The real question you should ask yourself is, do you have enough of what you need to start over?

19 **If you're stuck in a divorce battle over something, take a step back.** Try to see if there's a new way of approaching the problem. For example, if you and your former spouse are going back and forth over a valuable piece of art or jewelry, consider having both parties give up their claim to the object and putting it in a trust for your children.

20 **Choose a divorce lawyer carefully.** Make it clear that your attorney works for you, not the other way around. Some lawyers are more attuned to the emotional issues you will be facing than others. If you hire a lawyer who has a reputation for being adversarial, you may be inviting a war. (You may also skip the attorneys altogether, and consider mediation or other alternative dispute-resolution options.)

21 **Don't avoid financial questions in your divorce.** Usually, this stems from an attempt to keep things peaceful, but it can lead to conflicts and problems down the line. The longer you have been together and the older you are, the more complicated your financial division may be. One of the biggest financial mistakes divorcing couples make is overlooking taxes, social security, and retirement funds. Keep those in mind.

22 **Don't over-worry about how difficult your divorce will be for the children.** They'll be OK. Studies show that 75 to 85 percent of children cope quite well with their parents' divorces. Moreover, when parents have been fighting bitterly prior to the divorce, the adverse effects seem to be minimal—probably because the kids find the divorce to be a relief from the constant emotional stress of their parents fighting.

23 **Know what's in a name.** Researchers speculate that naming reflects parents' expectations for a child, and that teachers and fellow students reinforce stereotypes associated with names. Other children and teachers will treat boys and girls with certain names in certain ways. Girls with names that are rated as highly feminine, for example, tend to have lower scores in math and science; children as early as kindergarten will say that a boy named Colt is more "active" than one named Percival.

24 **Don't name your kid after a car.** Seriously. Once people get to know your amazing son or daughter, they will quickly form a more nuanced picture and develop a deep appreciation for his or her uniqueness. An unusual name isn't needed for that.

25 **With children in a blended family, keep introductions simple.** If a child hears an introduction that separates the biological children in the family from the stepchildren or adoptive children, his feelings might be hurt. Just say something like, "These are my kids," and then give their names.

26 **Give a brand-new mom a bit of space.** Unless you're a member of the immediate family, don't rush right over to see the new arrival—especially if Mom has had a difficult birth. Delay your visit for a few days, and when you do arrive to drop off a gift or to extend your congratulations, keep your visit to twenty minutes or less.

27 **If you're not part of the immediate family, don't worry about bringing a gift to a new parent.** That being said, it's certainly not wrong to do so, and will most likely be appreciated. Consider cooking some great meals that she can keep in her freezer and heat as needed.

28 **Support babies' heads when you're holding them.** Until they're six months old, babies don't have a lot of control over their heads and necks. When you do hand the child back to her parents, always present her bottom first, head last, and keep the head supported until you're sure someone else has it supported.

29 **Don't instigate sibling rivalry.** If you've brought a toy for the baby, bring something small for any sibling(s) as well, so they don't feel too jealous.

30 **Try not to jostle a baby too much.** If she's awake, try entertaining her by repeating silly noises. Keep it up as long as your sanity allows, and the baby will make satisfying happy noises unless she is hungry or tired, or needs a diaper change.

INDEX